Pretty Guardian
Sailor Moon
9

..... My dream is to be an idol!
..... My dream is to have a happy marriage and to open a cake shop!
..... My dream is to become a doctor.
..... My dream is to be head priest of Hikawa Jinja Shrine.

Pretty Guardian
Sailor Moon

Act 40 Dream 2, Mercury Dream

CONTENTS

Pretty Guardian SAILORMOON

...can't breathe...

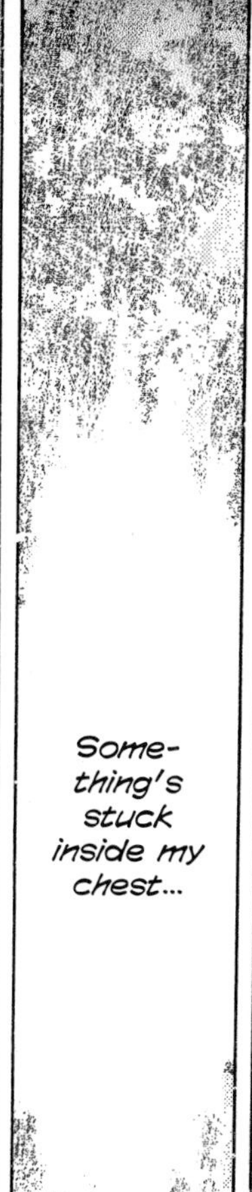

ZHAAA

J MEDICAL UNIVERSITY HOSPITAL
Mamo-chan...!

...Usa ...?
...Chibi-Usa...?

GLISTEN
Mamo-chan...?
...Thank goodness!

BAM
Usagi? Chibi-Usa?!
How's Mamoru-san?! We heard he collapsed and had to be taken away in an ambulance...!

Every-body!

WHIRL くるっ

Mamo-chan *just* opened his eyes. The doctor said it's nothing serious...

H-HUH?

...something feels a little off...

...come to think of it...

WHOOSH ばっっっ

That hair! BLACK LADY??!

Usagi suddenly shrank...
...and Chibi-Usa got bigger?!
WHAT ?!!
... Chibi-Usa?
Uh-huh.
... Usagi?
Yup.
The moment we transformed back, something crashed into us...
...and we ended up like this.
What "something"?!
Obviously we don't know! We have no idea why we ended up like this!
Was it an enemy?!
That's right! An enemy appeared when we ran after that tiger that had escaped from the circus!

The Dead Moon Circus ...!! I *knew* it...!
Huh? Come to think of it, where's Ami-chan?
KACHAK
Sorry I'm late.
How is Mamoru-san?
Chibi-Usa-chan?!
Figures Ami-chan would figure it out right away!
Whoa!!
...or
are you just dressing up like her, Usagi-chan?!
Messing around at a time like this!
...Ami-chan...! Waah...
What ?!
Your heights got re-versed?!
Sort of.
But neither of us is any different inside,
so it's like only our outward appear-ances changed.
That's terrible!

While we're here, let's get the two of you checked out, too!

... "While we're here?"

...Ami-chan?!

FACHAK

I just asked Mama to see that Mamoru-san gets examined.

She's an internist here at this hospital.

Ami?

They're ready to examine Chiba Mamoru-san.

That's Ami-chan's mom?!

She's so pretty!

Thanks for being so nice to Ami.

SMILE

We should have the results right away.

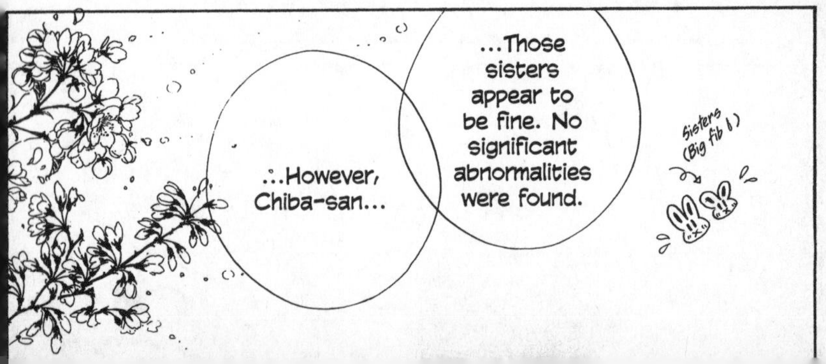

...Those sisters appear to be fine. No significant abnormalities were found.
...However, Chiba-san...
Sisters (Big fib)

...Shadows on my lungs?
Well... you see...
There are these shadows that I've never seen before, in areas you wouldn't expect to find them... I don't even know if "shadow" is the proper term for them.
This is the first time I've seen a case like this.
Have you suffered collapses like today often before?
It would be best to run more tests.
When can you return?
...Ah, in that case...
I'll find out when I can miss class...
and call to make an appointment.
...Shadows on my lungs?
Mamo-chan! How'd it go?
...Nothing unusual.
Did you get your results too?
...They were normal...
...I don't know whether to be happy or disappointed...

... Though
I have to say, you're really pretty all grown-up, Chibi-Usa.
Carefree Mamo-chan
BLUSH
I'm going!!
How?
We've got to get them back to their old selves!
Er, uh...
What if they're stuck like this for-ever?
No way!!
...I'll head home first and try to fool Ikuko-Mama and Kanji-Papa!
Because we can't go home like this!
Usagi, you take Mamo-chan home! I'll come pick you up once it's night-time!
Wow, so level-headed all of a sudden!
Chibi-Usa's such an adult!
Tsukino
...ガチャッ
GACHAK
...I'm home!
TIPTOE
Oh!
Is that you, Chibi-Usa-chan? Welcome home!
PATTER- PATTER
パタパタ

さっ
TOSS

ボワワン
BOIOING

Ahh, Usagi...
もぐ
MWOK
...ニコッ
SMILE
もぐ
MWOK
You're home late.
もぐ
MWOK

Usagi's Room
パタン
PATNK
...Somehow, I still feel a little guilty.
I'm sorry, Ikuko-Mama!
Still...
I have to say, you're really pretty.

くるりっ
WHIRL
...Eh heh heh! ♡
カシャン
KASHANK
はっ
AH!
リン
CHING

FWAA
...Young maiden.
Helios!
Your appearance...!
It looks like you've grown up!
...How beautiful!
You truly are the young maiden that I've been seeking...!!
H-Hold on!
You've got it wrong!
...You just suddenly grew bigger?
Yeah.
I bet this is our new enemy's black magic!
...That's what Luna said,
but what if we really *can't* ever return to normal?

Unfortunately, I currently do not possess the power to sense evil shadows.
...How-ever, I **can** tell you that this is quite like them...
...to put the two of you under such a spell.
"Them" who?!
Helios, you're familiar with—
—this enemy?
Who in the world...
...are you?
...My true form is...
FWSH
No...
I cannot say yet.
But young mai-den,
your aid is critical.
...Please believe me.

...Young maiden,
you hold the key that shall save me, no, everything.
...You who possess beautiful dreams...
...are protected by the light of the moon...
...and are both princess and guardian.
...O Chosen One, bearer of the sacred gem which undoes the Golden Crystal seal...
FFT
Helios?!
...So that's the young maiden Helios is searching for?
...Am I really...
...the one...?
I have to go to Mamo-chan's!
I have to tell them that Helios appeared!

Can I get you anything, Mamo-chan?
I'm fine, really.

Thanks to all the commotion, we ended up alone! ♡
The first time in a while! ♡
What luck! ♡

Usa?
WHA ?!
Wh- What is it?

Sorry to be sick...
...at such a difficult time.

...That circus troupe...

...The Dead Moon Circus...
I bet they've made this city their target.
We need to do something about them fast.
SMILE ニコッ
Yeah.
...S-Somehow, this throws everything off.
...Hey, Mamo-chan?
...Is it okay if I cuddled with you...
...just a bit?
Sure...
Eh heh heh! ♡
Whee! ♡
GLOM ぴとっ
STARE じっ
Now's my chance!
UH
HEH へラッ
...Don't worry,
I'm sure you'll return to normal in no time.

Feels like a crime
I-I can't do this, it's like I'm looking at Chibi-Usa...
Darn it...! We're all by ourselves for once, and I just can't get in the mood!
PAT PAT なでなで
With that way-too-long spring finally over, I was hoping to take our relationship to the next level!
Why'd I end up like this?! What am I gonna do if I can't get back to how I was before?!
...I feel like Chibi-Usa is always
SOB くっすん
interfering with our relationship somehow.
Usa, that's a bit much, don't you think?
SNIFF
...Sorry. My bad.
You know that Chibi-Usa gets lonely really easily.
I'm sure she's just barely holding in her despair at not being able to return to the thirtieth century.
She even put on a brave face just now.
It was so sweet of her.
Especially considering that her flaky mother has gotten tinier.
Say what?

Don't worry, I won't make Chibi-Usa feel hopeless!
The enemy has shown up now, so I'll protect her, no matter what!
Leave it to me!
...!
Mamo-chan?!
... I'm fine.
I'm going to rest a bit.
Usa...
...I keep ending up being a weight on your shoulders.
...not only do I lack even a fraction of your power,
but I'm always dragging you down.
...We know what our future looks like, right?

Yet I some-times feel...
...that I'm just going to get in the way of your glittering dreams and your future...
...forever.
...Oh, Mamo-chan...
...we can always
change the future, you know,
as much as we want to.
I'm the one who keeps getting you involved by being near you.
...Making you have such paniful thoughts...
Maybe it's me who shouldn't be near you.
...But my dream,
Mamo-chan...

...is just to be at your side...
like this...
...forever and ever.
That's my only dream...
...I know...
...that no matter how much I love him,
Mamo-chan is my Papa in the future.
And that Mamo-chan has Usagi.
KRIIK
...キィ
Small Lady...
ROLL
コロッ
...I'm not that small right now.
GLANCE
ちろっ

... Lady ...
That's acceptable!
But for sure ...
...even if it *is* due to the enemy's black magic, you've grown up so splendidly...!
If Their Majesties were to see you like this, they'd be so proud...
SHIMMER
うる
SHIMMER
うる
Fine, so the normal me is a shrimp.
You're a meanie, Diana!
Ah ha ha, sorry, sorry!
My dream is to one day become a real adult.
...To become a lovely, wonderful lady.
And to someday
meet my own one and only
Prince...

SUU
Prince ...
FWAA
... Please forgive me...
...For not being able to protect Elysion.
And not just Elysion...
...but your body as well...
I beg you to find it.
The Golden Crystal...

...my Prince.
BLINK

...A dream...?

Mizuno

CLICK
CLACK

BEEP
BEEP
What the ...?!

What is this strange aura en-veloping the Jûban shopping district,
with that circus troupe at the center ...?!

Is it a ward?!
The Dead Moon Circus's doing?!
When did they —?!

...Ami...
Train yourself so that you can always be on guard against the enemy and always make calm judgements.
Plus, have confidence in yourself so that everyone can rely on you with peace of mind.
If you just close your eyes...
...the correct answer will always be waiting inside you.
For you are everyone's brain.
Se-tsu-na-san...
...Sailor Pluto...
She was so great, and she knew everything...
She taught us so many important things.
But she's not here anymore.
...I can't lean on her...
I have to be strong!

If they really are enemies, I know they'll attack again!

In any case, we need to protect the residents of Jûban. That's the top priority.

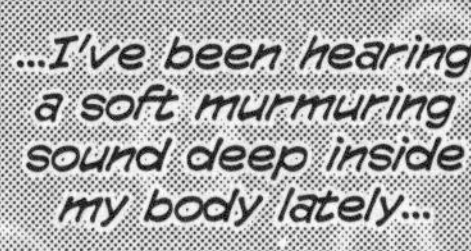

...I've been hearing a soft murmuring sound deep inside my body lately...

How mysterious...
I sense a flow of water...

Mama?
GACHANK
You're still up? It's past one.

Welcome back. You're home late.
There was an emergency at the hospital. I'm ex-hausted.
Are you hungry? Have you eaten?

I fixed myself something earlier, so I'm fine. Don't worry.

...You're so level-headed and mature.
But I always take advantage of that and leave you home alone. I'm a bad mother.
I'm wrong to neglect my own household,
and devote my attention to a career saving others.
Mama...
...My Papa is a Japanese painter.
His love of leisure and nature took him on constant sketching trips.
He didn't have anything in common with Mama.
...One day, Papa decided to seclude himself inside his studio in the woods...
and never came back.
*Notification of Divorce
To this day, Papa always sends me a postcard on my birthday.
I recall Papa also mentioning that I was so levelheaded that I didn't seem like a child.
CHUCKLE
クスッ

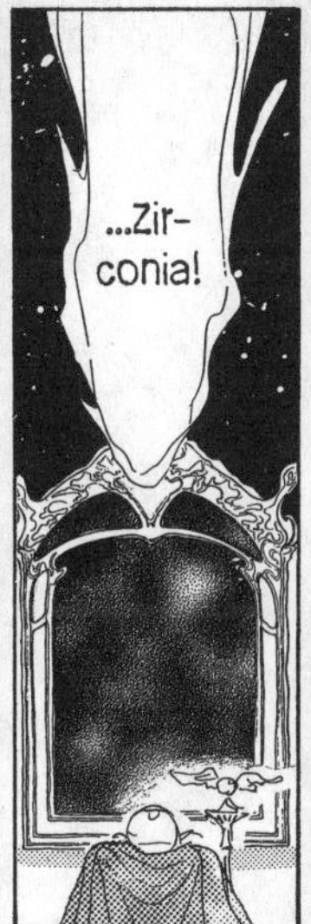
...Zirconia!

Now that we know that those of the
Kingdom of the White Moon have been reborn into this world,
we cannot just leave them be!

I am well aware of that!
Nehelenia-sama!

WHOOSH!

Girlies!

The power those Moon Kingdom girls used to kick around our Lemures...

That is the very power...

...of that sacred gem that tortured our Dead Moon clan back in ancient times.

The Moon Kingdom's crystal of infinite power, the "Legendary Silver Crystal"!

We cannot rule this world until we obliterate them!

First, make them fall victim to nightmares!

Heh heh

Eradicate everything that contains light! That is the way of the Dead Moon Circus!

Cackle cackle

Hee hee ♡
Zirconia-sama?
Please allow me...
...Fish's Eye, to do it! ♡

Now, mirror, my dear mirror! ♡ Please show me. ♡
Those living in a city of plentiful dreams.
Those who posses light.

Those of the Kingdom of the White Moon...
...and those who protect them.

... Found one!
One who can manipulate the flow of water, just like me,
and who possesses beautiful dreams.

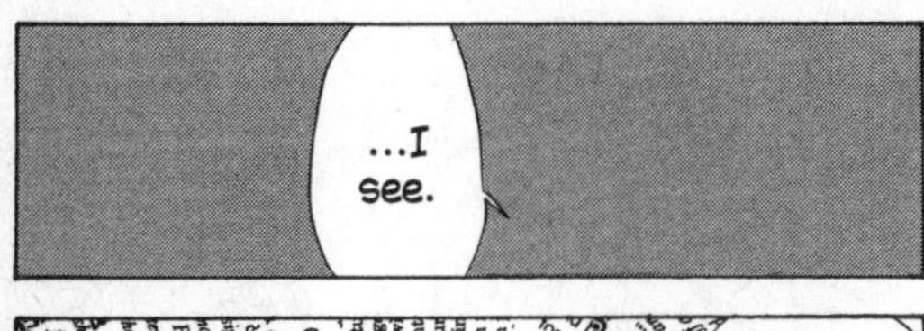
...I see.

So, no changing back once morning came, huh?
Ami-chan!!
Waaah
I guess the "maybe you'll return to your old selves the next day" fairy tale ending was too much to hope for.

Anyways, we're both gonna fake being sick today so we can stay home from school.
WEEP
WEEP
...I need to help the two of them right away.
CHING
PLIP
PLIP
SHAA
...The Dead Moon Circus...
SHIVER
Exactly what kind of people are they?
NO TRESPASSING
A tropical fish store, here?
FISH
Discus Farm
Discus Farm

...How pretty!

I feel like I'm in the water with them.

You look so happy.

When you feel drawn to water...

...it means you're really stressed.

It's a sign of pent up frus-tration.

Would you like to purchase a pet fish, perhaps?

I recom-mend this one.

Hee hee, it *is* cute! ♡

It looks like the one on Papa's post-card, too.

Discus Farm

Thank you very much! ♡

Yep, maybe Mama might enjoy it as well.

HO HO ふふっ ♡

I wonder if Mama will be sur-prised.
I wish I could show it to her right now.

zzz すぅっ
CLUB コポ
CLUB コポ

GACHANK ...ガチャン
Hmm ...?
KACHAA カチャ
Mama?

ドキン BA-BUMP
...Isn't your daughter still awake?
...Mama?
B-BMP ...ドキン
B-BMP ...ドキン

くすくす SNICKER
That child's only interested in studying. We have nothing to do with each other.

...Mama?!

OH!

FFT

Isn't that me?!

Papa, Papa!

Ami, please don't tag along anymore.

Papa's really tired...

...of your Mama, and of you.

You're only interested in studying. Your pleading won't change my mind.

Good-bye.

Papa!

No! Why can't you understand?

I'm always thinking so much about the both of you!

Usagi-chan?!
FFT
?!
We're really happy just like this.
The three of us are always together.
You don't need to hold it in.
You were jealous of those three, weren't you?
SUU
...Hey...
PASHAA
We don't need anything or anyone else.

Admit the truth.
...That's right, I've always been lonely.
SUU
SNICKER
My dream is to be loved
by someone. Anyone at all...
NOO!!
VWATCH
You're wrong! That's a lie!
Help! Mama!
Mama?!
No! That's not Mama!
Snap out of it, Ami!!
This is all an illusion!
CHIT-CHITTER
CACKLE CACKLE
CLATTER

CHITTER
WHOOSH
CACKLE
!!
The enemy?!
Here, inside my apartment?!
WHOOSH!
I've got to let Usagi-chan know...!
Usagi-chan! Can you hear me?!
Ami-chan?!
It's the enemy!!
WHOOSH
!!
CHIT-CHITTER
CACK-CACKLE
Ami-chan?!
DWOM
...I'm always relying on somebody else...
...This is a nightmare.
ZWUB
?!

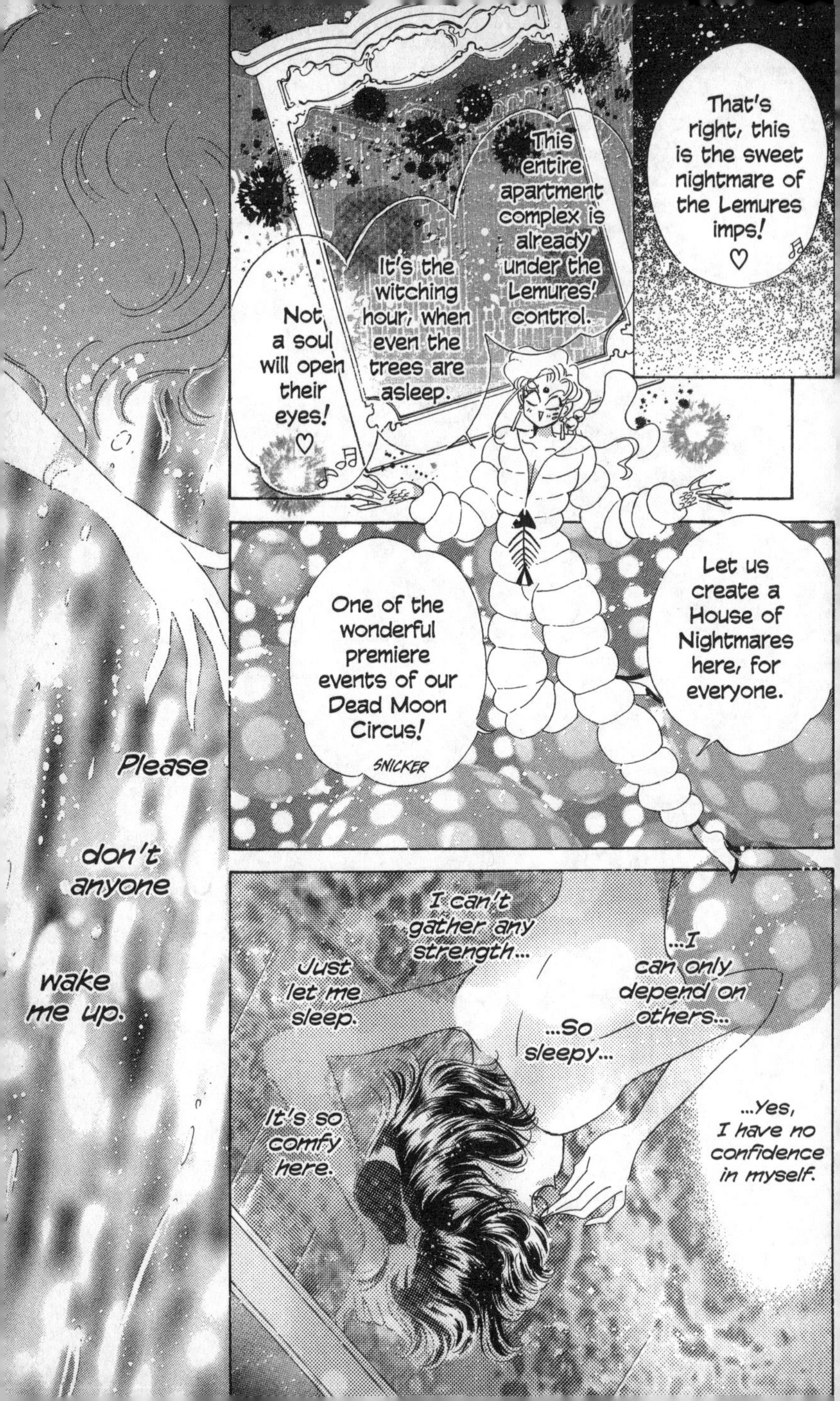
That's right, this is the sweet nightmare of the Lemures imps! ♡
This entire apartment complex is already under the Lemures' control.
It's the witching hour, when even the trees are asleep.
Not a soul will open their eyes! ♡
Let us create a House of Nightmares here, for everyone.
One of the wonderful premiere events of our Dead Moon Circus!
SNICKER
...I can only depend on others...
I can't gather any strength...
Just let me sleep.
...So sleepy...
...Yes, I have no confidence in myself.
It's so comfy here.
Please
don't anyone
wake me up.

...Prin-
cess...

...Princess
Mercury!

...Who's
there?

...Who's
calling to
me...?

...My true dream...?

...Aah...
...that's right.
I've got
tons of people I love
in my life.
I want to love them a lot, lot more.
...I want to protect them.
That's why I'm studying.
And
my dream
is...

For that is my mission!
PAAA
SPLASH
What the?!
...to become a full-fledged guardian and protect every-one!
...The glow of this blue brooch!
Mercury Crystal Power Make Up!!
PAAAN

I am the Mercury Harp.
A lyre ?!
Now! Kick aside the nightmare!
It has a will of it's own?!
Mercury Aqua Rhapsody!!
PAA

CRACK
FFT
FFT
Mama!
WHUD
... Unh ...
BAMM
Mercury!
Usagi-chan! Chibi-Usa-chan!

Sink or swim!
We've got to transform, Chibi-Usa!
Yup!
Moon Crisis!!
Make Up!!
VCCH
VCCH

PAAA
Super Sailor Moon!!
Super Sailor Chibi Moon!!

Let's do this, Chibi Moon!! *Moon Gorgeous Meditation!!*
PAAAA
SPLAT
Fish's Eye!!
They broke through my
Inversion Orb spell and transformed?!
How interesting!

Mercury!!
Super Sailor Moon! And Chibi Moon!
I'm so glad! You're back to normal...!
Yes! We did it, Chibi Moon!
GUTS!
Super Sailor Moon takes down the enemy in a flash each and every time...
...She really is strong...!
Usagi's strong and beautiful and everyone always needs her.
...That's right, every-one's lost without Usagi.

I've sensed it all along.

Even if I possess the same "Legendary Silver Crystal" and the exact same items as her...

...I can't draw their power on my own, without Sailor Moon.

I'm totally useless by my-self...!

Twinkle Yell!!

Chibi Moon?!

FWAA

Young maiden.

Helios,
I think you're wrong.
I don't
have a strong heart, or power, or a beautiful figure like Sailor Moon...!
I'm *not* the young maiden...
...that you seek, Helios!
The young maiden you seek? Helios?
...The young maiden...
...that I seek...

...is a princess-guardian who possesses beautiful dreams,
and is protected by the light of the moon.
...She is also the Chosen One who bears the sacred gem,
which undoes the seal upon the Golden Crystal...
A princess-guardian protected by the light of the moon.
...Golden Crystal?
That's right... I knew immediately, the moment I heard Helios utter those words.
...Don't tell me that maiden is... Sailor Moon?
...Or rather, Princess Serenity?

...Then, Super Sailor Moon, you...
...are Princess Serenity?
I'm not the young maiden that Helios is seeking...
I'm not the one he needs...
Chibi Moon?!

Pretty Guardian
Sailor Moon
Act 41 Dream 3,
Mars Dream

Chibi Moon!!
SUU
Helios!
SST

...I'm so stupid.
...I mean, I knew it.

...Then, Super Sailor Moon, you...
...are Princess Serenity?
THROB

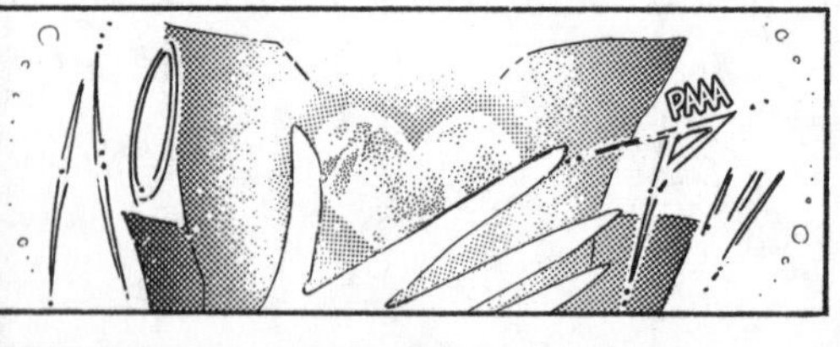
PAAA

Usagi was actually...
...the maiden that Helios was seeking...
...not me.
SNIFF
...That hurts.

Aah...
...it's not like running away...
...or losing my nerve is going to change anything.

Please call me.

I thought I could still be useful.

Please lend me your strength.

Young maiden...

It was so wonderfully flattering to be called that.

SWU
スワッ

CHING

...But I'm not good enough, after all.

Pint-sized, powerless me...

A princess-guardian who possesses beautiful dreams and is protected by the light of the moon.

A maiden who bears the sacred gem which undoes the seal upon the Golden Crystal...

...
Helios...
...do you think...
...that the day
will come when people will need me, too...?
I won-der...
...if my dreams will ever
come true...
...that I'll grow up
to be a great guard-ian...
...and a lovely lady...?
PLIP
PLIP
Chibi-Usa what?!

A storm's coming!
Let's go look for her!
Chibi-Usa ...!!
SHAAA
NUZZLE
すりっ

...Do not
cry, little
maiden.

It is thanks to your asisstance...
...that Super Sailor Moon can now fight at full strength.
Everyone's worried about you and they're searching for you right now.
...You are someone...
...who is always dearly needed.

You are surround-ed...
...by overflowing love.
...This is the long-est...
...I can maintain this form...
Little maid-en...
SW
I promise to come visit you again.
So please don't cry...
SST

Chibi-Usa!
Oh, phew ...!
You'll catch a cold.
Let's go home.
Chibi-Usa?
... Where's Helios?
He disappeared right after you left.
We never finished our con-versation.
ドキン BA-BMP
...Helios?
...That was Helios just now...?
ドキン BA-BMP
ドキン BA-BMP

FWAA
……ふわっ……
HAHH
…はあ
HAHH
…はあ
…Ho.
ZLITHER
…ズルッ
Quite impressive, that you managed to escape...
...my binding curse.
ZLITHER
…ズルッ

How-ever...
...both you and this land are already mine.
And eventually all of the surface world shall also be mine.
I won't allow you to interfere... heh heh heh.
...This land and my body may be yours...
HAH
...but you don't have any control over my heart yet!
HAH
The Prince and Princess shall definitely eradicate...
...an evil like you!
Inso-lence!
VRSSH
...I must find the Golden Crystal quickly...
...and restore this land, or else...
...the planet itself will be...

POHH
...
Aah!
No matter how often I look upon it, this planet is always as beautiful as a crystal ball...!
Here and now...
...our time is finally coming, Zirconia.
The White Moon Kingdom's light...
...no longer exists over there.
And without the White Moon Kingdom's protection...
...this planet, and the reborn denizens of the Moon Kingdom, are like newborn babes.
The time has come...
...for us to obtain this planet and their sacred gem, the "Legendary Silver Crystal,"
with its infinite power.
But Nehelenia-sama,
it is said...
...that the crystal can only be used by its true owner...

Zir-conia!

Those words of yours...

You do know that you're speaking to the Dead Moon's beautiful and mighty...

...Queen Nehelenia, do you not?

Please forgive me!

You are the true Queen of the Moon,
the true owner of the Moon Kingdom's sacred gem...
...the "Legendary Silver Crystal," and the exalted one who shall take everything unto herself.

Heh heh heh!
Heh heh heh!

T·A Acadmy for Girls
Middle School
High School
T·A Acadmy for Girls
TNK
Hino.

What's going on? Your arrows lack confidence today.

Rei-chaaaan! ☆ When you act the way you are right now...
How to Run a Shrine
...you look just like Ami-chan...! ☆

Eh?!
"How to Run a Shrine?"

Grandpa caught a cold and can't get out of bed right now. Plus, we're in an economic downturn.

I'm looking for efficient management techniques.
Why don't you hire some-one?

No!
That would add labor costs!

Our philosophy is to avoid all un-neccessary expenses.
Rei-chan!
Rei-chan, I've got the perfect suggestion! ♡ You ought to...
...get a husband! ♡
A hus-band?!
You've *got* to be kidding! Why the heck would I do that?!
I know quite well that you hate boys, Rei-chan, Mm-hmm.
The point is...
...just don't think of it as your getting married,
but as having someone marry into your family to work at the shrine for free. ♡
Minako's Nice Idea
Of course, let that person take over running the shrine from your grandpa, too,
and have him do all the day-to-day work,
leaving you to do whatever you want. ♡
Just think of him as your lackey, Rei-chan!
It's a great concept! Go hubby!
Lackey... ♡ That doesn't sound too bad... ♡
...seems cozy! ♡
... Both of you,
can't you talk more like stu-dents?

Speaking of student stuff...
GASSH
Aah, I wanna boyfriend!!
...Not again!
What? It's right for a high school girl to want a boyfriend!
DEAD MOON CIRCUS
circus
Tomorrow is...
...the Dead Moon Circus' opening day!
Sorry to interrupt your super-serious discussion, but...
Luna, Artemis, Diana! ♡
We're going in, every-one!
Just you wait, Dead Moon Circus!
Ready when you are!

Hikawa Shri
The fact that I can't kick this fever must mean I'm approaching my end... Namu Amida Butsu*...
MUTTER MUTTER
UNGH うーん
うーん UNGH
...Grandpa, we're a Shinto shrine, not a Buddhist temple... ☆
*Namu Amida Butsu = Buddhist prayer
Well, let your granddaughter and heir...
...handle things for a while, and get some rest.
Excuse us!
Could we please have two matchmaker charms?! ♡
Sure. That'll be 800 yen*.
Thank you! ♡
*About $10 US.
I'm going to give mine to my sempai! ♡
I hope he feels the same way! ♡

Are boyfriends really such desirable commodities?!
We want BFs!!
My dream is to be a bride! ♡
My dream is to go into medicine!
Mine is to become an idol!
...I...
...want to take over Hikawa Shrine from Grandpa and become its head priestess.
And I'll just stay right here.
Though a bit uncertain, I just had a feeling it was the natural thing to do.
Everyone else has such a clear idea of what they want.
FLAP
...My dream...

Your arrows lack confidence today.
FLAFF
FLAFF
KAW
FLAFF
FLAFF
HURL
Come! Phobos! Deimos!
...It was before she started grade school that Rei first came to this shrine, I reckon.
A-Ha ha ha

KAW
KAW
There are crows in your garden, Grandpapa?
There are lots of crows in Tokyo.
Particularly in Shinjuku and Roppongi. Is this an unusual sight for you?
OH!
はっ
DAA
FLAFF
FLAFF
Phobos! Deimos!
Eh?!
Rei?!
These two...
...are named Phobos and Deimos.
It just came to me, but I'm sure of it.
She was always a wondrous girl.
...But I know...

That one day, Rei, you shall...
...leave here...
...and fly off to that place where you were always meant to be.

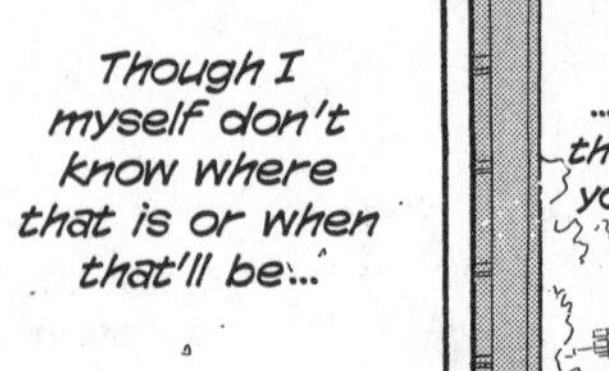

Though I myself don't know where that is or when that'll be...

DEAD MOON CIRCUS

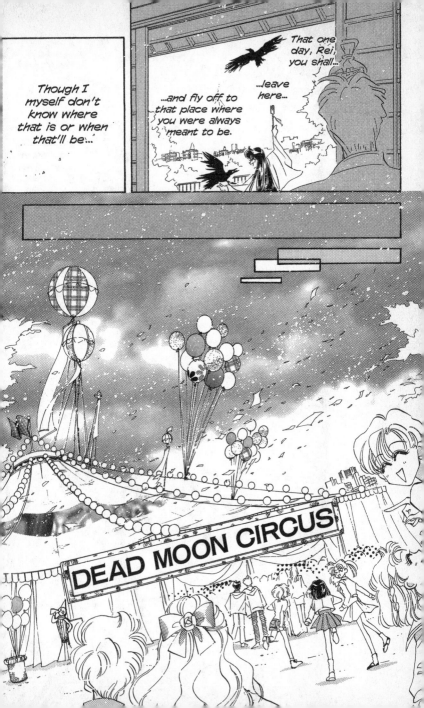

Wow!

The Great Dead Moon Circus Show...!

Buy your same-day tickets here!

Even those who won't be seeing the show,

come in and enjoy our traveling amusement park! ♡

GAH!
The S-section seats are 10,000 yen* each?!
How pricey! That's unbelievable!
I thought the yen was strong the world over?!
What a scam! I'm even more suspicious of the Dead Moon Circus now!!
Tee hee hee! ♡

*About $125 US.

Whee! ♡ I wanna eat soft serve! I wanna ride a rollercoaster! ♡
Now, now, Chibi-Usa! We didn't come here to play! ☆

I'm going to take a lap and have a look around. The rest of you stay here.
Okaaay! ♡
I heard there's a haunted house!
And a wax museum!
Let's check them out! ♡
Hey, Mamo-chan, can we go ride the go-karts for a bit? Please?! ♡
Sure!
Oooh, me too, me too! ♡
This is kind of a let-down.
I mean, I even brought Phobos and Deimos along because I was so nervous
about what incredible malefic energy we might encounter. ☆
It's been so long since I felt like this!
So exciting! So thrilling!
I feel like I've become a kid again!

MIRROR HOUSE
...Mirror House?

RRORHOUSE

SST

FFT

MIRROR HOUSE

KAW

KAW

The show is about to begin!
Right this way!
Please hurry!
BZZZZZZZ

Where's Luna and the others?
Huh? Rei-chan's missing, too!

Oh! There they come!
DAA
Don't leave us behind!

Hey there!

No cats allowed inside!
POI

No waaay!!

WOOOW
わあああ
Now, shall I feed these humans to my darling Lemures?
Or shall I make them into faithful minions?
WOWW
わああ
HEH HEH
クスクス
WOW
わあっ
I'm feeling dizzy, like my head's spinning.
Feels so gooood!
So fun!
That reminds me, where's Rei-chan?
Beats me. She's probably around here somewhere.
SWIRL

Shoot! <> My vertigo's getting a lot worse.
Hey, everybody, let's go grab some fresh air... The exit's...
WAVR

...Huh?
... That's weird ...!

There's no...
...exit any-where?!

CHIT-CHITTER
CRCK-CRCKLE

CLATTER
CLATTER
CLATTER

Mirrors that don't reflect anything ...?
I wonder what the trick behind that is.

Don't worry! There's no trick or secret to it!

...Is *that* me?!

Nice to meet you, "me!"

No! Is this an enemy trick...?!

くすくす
HEH HEH

Now then! Let me project the inside of your heart onto these mirrored walls here.

You already know this, but...

...Mama died when I was really young...

...and Papa is so busy with his government job...

...that he's pretty much dumped me off to grandpa.

I've been unhappy since I was little, right?

That's why I've always wanted to be happy.
DOM
I can't get out! I'm trapped?! When did they—?!
The truth is, it's real tiresome getting abused by Usagi,
and being forced to hang out...
...with Ami, Makoto, and Minako.
I'm *fed up* with them!
Stop it!
F-E-D U-P!
I do *not* think that!
F-E-D U-P!
I want to start putting *my* happiness, *my* needs first. I've got to make some friends...
...who'll always listen to what *I* say.
...That's right! ♡ Like a boyfriend who's totally crazy for me, for example! ♡

Evil Spirit...
BWOO
FFT
...be exorcised!!
VASSH
悪霊退散*
PISH
PISSH
*"Evil Spirit Be Exorcised"
FFT
Feh!
HAHH
...はあ
HAHH
はあ
How careless of you!
Tiger's Eye!
しゅん
DROOP
Whiiine
悪霊退散
Oohoo! ♡
Still, the magic that I, PallaPalla, cast upon the Mirror House...
...the "Orb Evanescence," cannot be shaken, much less broken, by such a puny move!

SUU
...Well, I suppose that every once in a while...
...I'll kiss a man or two that I'm not really into.
!!
But the end goal...
...is to marry someone rich ♡ and live comfortably for the rest of my life!
That's what happiness is to a girl! ♡
The high priestess of a shrine? Give me a break!
I must transform!! There's no point in staying here!
Mars Star Power Make...
KINN

VRSSH
VRSSH
Argh!

I can't trans-form?!
No...
Maybe I got the transfor-mation spell wrong?!
Transfor-mation...?
What transfor-mation...?
FFT
I... what's my dream...?
What was I looking for, again?

SNIFF SNIFF
しくしく
I so wanted to see the circus show!
I am sick and tired of this!
It's always like this! So we're cats, so what?!☆
GRAWW
GRAWW
Phobos and Deimos sure are raucous today.
OH!
PING
Hey!
Look at that, Luna!
...The tent's entrance and exit flaps have vanished ?!
Oh no!
MIRROR HOUSE
GRAWR
GRAWW
Phobos?! Deimos?!

ROR HOUSE
GASHAAN
SHAA
KAK
...Mars!

Princess Mars!
... Who?
SST
...Who are you ...?!

FFT
... Everybody ?!
Oh no!!
I've got to help them!!
How could I have left them...!
...Something happened to me! I was deceived by the enemy and beset with doubt...
I've got to be strong !!
Now that's much more like our Princess Mars!
SMILE
OH!
...You two!
You can't be...
I'm Phobos!
And I'm Deimos...
Now transform!
Here is your Mars Crystal.

My Crystal!
The Mars Crystal!!
FFT
Phobos?! Deimos?!
And take them out with a single Mars Arrow!
Mars Crystal Power Make Up!!
...Aah! I feel flames rushing through my entire body!
I don't know why I was wavering. I am the Guardian of Fire who pledged her chastity to Princess Serenity!
This is the sensation I've been seeking!
In order to protect the Princess, this planet, and my companions...

...This is...
...my Mars Arrow!!
Rei...
You are in possession of superbly honed nerves and senses.
Keep your channels wide open at all times.
And if you should still find yourself at the mercy of an enemy...
Draw a single string,
taut across your heart,
and with all your body and soul...
I will fight!! That is my raison d'être and my dream!

...let loose your killing arrow!!
Mars Flame Sniper!
VWOM
SHA
PSSH
PSSH
!!

FFT
!!
Tiger's Eye!!
WHOOSH
The Mirror House and Tiger's Eye were de-feated?!
WHOOSH
The exit's back ?!
SM
No! ☆ Foiled again!
Tiger's Eye!
I think
it was kinda interesting,
but kinda sleep-inducing, too?
Could I have fallen asleep? I don't remember much.
ぼ" DAZE
?
?
?
?
ざわ CHATTER
ざわ CHATTER

Every-body?!
Are you all right?!
That was really fun!
Rei-chan?! Luna, Artemis, and Diana!

Ehh?!
The entrances and exits had van-ished?!
The enemy showed up and you were fighting them?!

When I passed by the Mirror House, I was suddenly drawn to it...
And if you show any doubt, they shove their way right into the depths of your heart.
That's how nasty this enemy is!

They may be targeting us.
We need to be careful!

They're using their circus show to brainwash people...?!
...This is bad!

Dead Moon Circus!

At this rate, they'll succeed!

We need to do something!

Like expose their true identity, somehow!

And protect the residents of this city!

DEAD MOON CIRCUS

We must purge this city of the Dead Moon Circus as soon as possible!

Darn Sailor Guardians!
They're annoying ninnies, just as we'd heard!
I can't believe they took down first Fish's Eye,
and now Tiger's Eye, so easily!
Our show was interrupted, too!
They'll pay a high price for this!
But say we engage them directly in a frontal attack,
and they destroy the circus...
...we're the ones who that old hag
will shred to bits! ☆
In-deed! ♡
We must plan slowly, carefully, all while having fun! ♡
That's the best way to do it! ♡
For our Dead Moon Circus' show...
...has just barely begun! ♡

"...Do not cry...
...little maiden!"

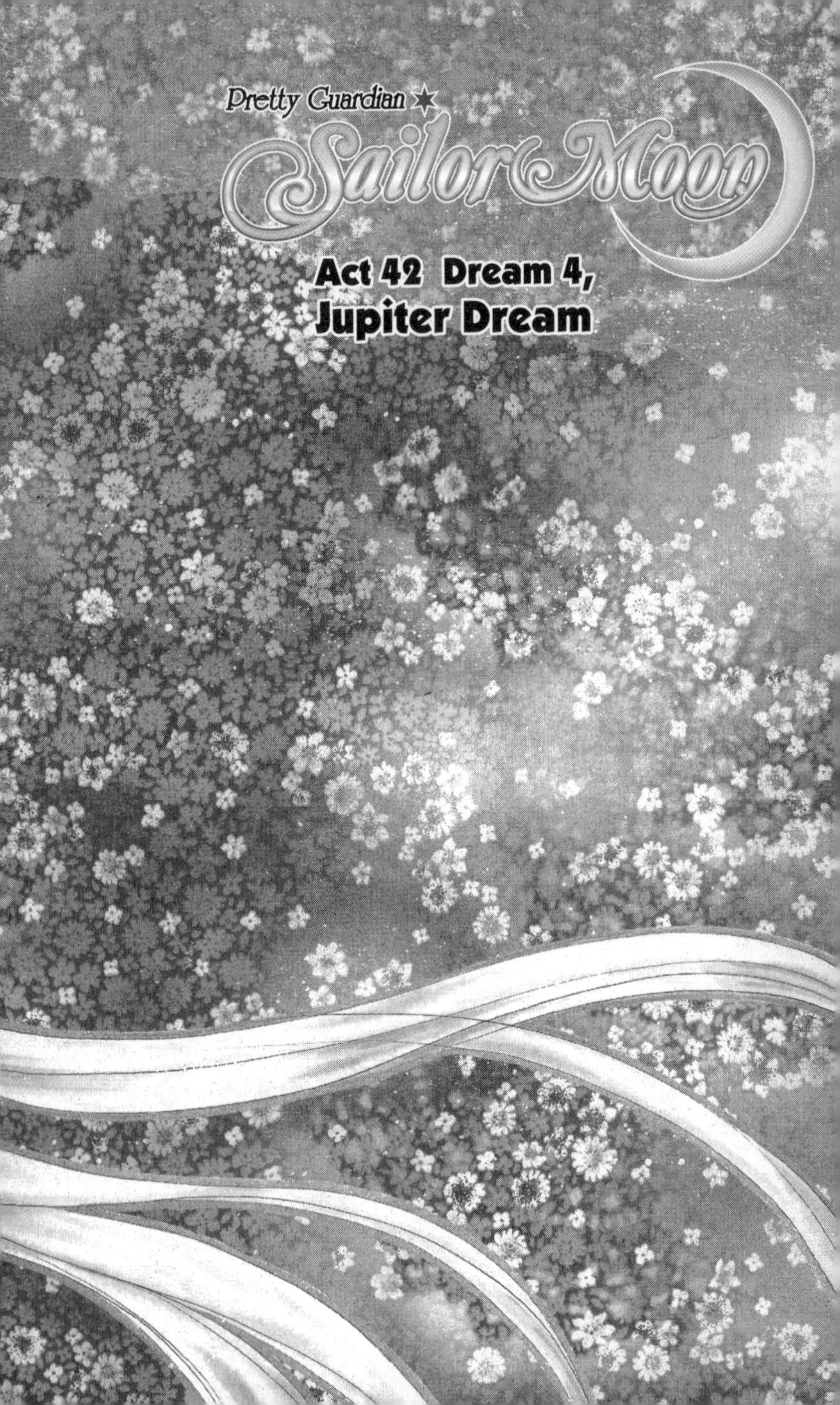
Pretty Guardian
Sailor Moon
Act 42 Dream 4,
Jupiter Dream

"...Do not cry...
...little maiden!"
...Helios...
...hasn't shown up again since then.
SILENCE
...はあー SIGH
Chibi-Usa...! Aren't you gonna eat your snack?

...I have no appetite, 'cuz I'm full of worries.
EHHH ?!
I see. That's too bad!
Because we have lemon pie, melon, chocolate cake, and even sherbet today...
...
DA DA DA DA DA
...はあ はあ
HAHH HAHH
I'm not hungry...
... but I'll eat.
Okay, sure.
...
You going some-where?
Mamo-chan's.

Mamo-chan's been feeling sick and staying home from college all this time.
I was thinking of visiting him. Wanna come along?
Oh!
Nope.
That's okay.
I've decided to stop getting in the way of the two of you.
Have fun!
What's gotten into you??
Is a catastrophic event about to occur?!

Despite already having a soulmate, Mamo-chan...
...I'm so bad...
B-BMP B-BMP
...ドキドキ

...all I can think about since that moment... is Helios.

I feel like I'm committing adultery, like I'm CHEATING on him!
SOB
Note: ADULTERY An illicit love affair with someone who is married and has kids!
Not to be confused with "eating!"
Though neither party is married and has kids, in this case.
Helios...
Why did you suddenly stop appearing?
Was that your true form, Helios?
Why do you have the appearance of a pegasus?
...You seem full of mysteries and secrets, Helios.
...I want to help you.
...Maybe I should go talk about this with someone.
I'm just wasting time worrying and thinking about it on my own.

I envy Usagi.
She's got so many friends to ask for advice.
Small Lady! ☆ You're still young and in training!
You cannot compare yourself to Usagi-sama! It's not proper!
I know!
...One day, I'm gonna become a full-fledged guardian too,
and have my own team of companions... I really hope so...
...I have to be strong!
HAHH はぁ
HAHH はぁ
If I don't stay strong...
even the Prince's body might be compromised...

And this planet, too...

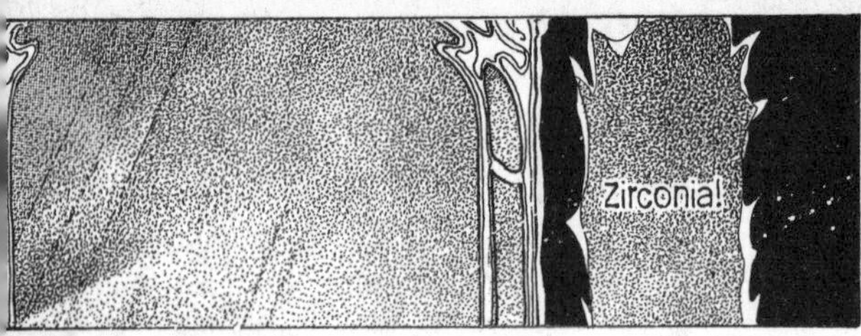

Zirconia!

Yes, Nehelenia-sama?

...Who am I?

You are this world's greatest beauty and intellect...
...the noble Queen Nehelenia-sama,
foremost among the Dead Moon and our mistress of supreme power!

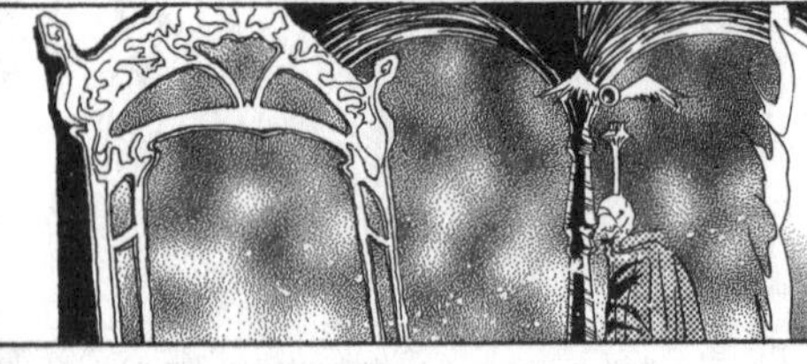

...And what is our deepest desire?

...Our dearest wish...
...is to make that sacred gem, the "Legendary Silver Crystal,"
and this green planet, ours...
...in place of the detestable White Moon Kingdom's Silver Millennium.
...And to eventually become the grand rulers of the entire universe.
Heh heh heh, that's right!
...Elysion has already fallen under our control.
That White Moon Kingdom too, which protected this planet for millennia...
...has already breathed its last breath and is now a dead satellite. Heh heh heh.
All that remains to be done is to get rid of those disgusting Moon Kingdom survivors.

Hurry!

I can't wait to see this green planet...
...full of nightmares and dark-ness...

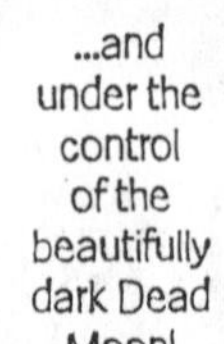
...and under the control of the beautifully dark Dead Moon!

Queen Nehe-lenia.
Please allow us...
...the Amazoness Quartet, to perform that task!

With our Amazon Stones!
PAAN

And these Lemures!
CHIT-CHITTER
HEH HEH HEH
We swear to take and make this planet our own!
CRCK-CRCKLE
Heh heh heh!

HAHH
... はあ
HAHH
はあ
SW
スラ
The aura around the Master's body has weakened.
...Abnormal phenomena are occurring inside it...
COUGH
COUGH
... However ...
There is nothing more that we can accomplish with our power...

ピンポーン
DING DONG
はっ
GASP
FFT
フッ
Mamo-chan?
... Usa...
I'm sorry, were you sleeping? I didn't mean to wake you.
How are you feeling?
ガサ
RUSTLE
ガサ
RUSTLE
I was worried that you might not be eating, so I brought you a bento.
I had Mama pack you plenty of *nimono**!
Also, I thought you might not be getting outside,
so I brought drinks and medicine...
...Usa.

*Japanese stewed dishes.

...Could you please go home?
...I was just thinking of going back to sleep.
...I need my rest...
...Oh!
Yeah.
I- I'm so sorry!
I- I'll be going now.
I apologize...
for barging in like that.
...Get some rest, okay?
Later!
PATANK
...!!
...I just can't let Usa find out!
COUGH
COUGH

...About this black blood!
"There are shadows on your lungs..."
COUGH
COUGH
What the heck is wrong with me?!
Dead Moon is about to make a magical move on this city...!
This is the worst possible time!
COUGH
COUGH
Am I going to end up dragging Usa down yet again...?!
...Mamo-chan...?!

WOWW
わあああっっ
CHATTER
ざわ
CHATTER
ざわ
What did you think of today's show?
I thought the elephant act and the motocycle show were particularly potent today.
I feel like they were emitting intense amounts of suspicious EM waves.
SHUFFLE
ぞろ
SHUFFLE
ぞろ
My head's spin-ning!
Are the other audience members okay?
Yeah, they all seem fine to the naked eye.
That was so much fun!
Totally incred-ible!
Let's come again!

...Ever since that day,

we've been coming by daily to scout the Dead Moon Circus.

I wonder if they're going to try to keep passing for an ordinary circus troupe?

Evidence is mounting that you're trying to brainwash folks with suspicious EM waves, Dead Moon! I swear I'll rip off your disguise!

But there've been no further enemy attacks since then. ☆

DEAD MOON CIRCUS

And no obvious change to the circus, either. ☆

I guess all that's left is to detain the circus folk one by one.

Exactly who and what is the enemy?

I wonder what kind of folks they are?

...We're not so dumb as to get pinned down that easily! ♡

Especially since we've heard rumors...
...of how incredibly fearsome you all are...
SST
...Sailor Guardians, you protectors of Silver Millennium!
We finally made it outside, something we'd only dreamed about.
So we're gonna have as much fun as we can! ♡
Heh heh!
BYON
GAN
OWW!
GONN
KYAA!
??
SNICKER
HEH HEH

Circus Sale!
DEAD MOON CIRCUS
The Circus Is In Town
The Circus Is In Super
SALE
DEAD MOON CIRCUS
DEAD MOON CIRCUS
Even so...
...the circus sure has become fully entrenched in this city.
I wonder if they're intending to stay here permanently?
Jûban's gotten kind of dirty since the circus arrived.
DEAD MOON CIRCUS
People congregate here. It can't be helped.
Once summer arrives, even more people will flock to the circus.
We need to do something before that.
It's so hot already.
This summer looks to be a scorcher.

Later
Bye-bye!
See you tomorrow!

キキッ
CHIT-CHITTER
ケケケッ
CACK-CACKLE
キキッ
CHIT-CHITTER

Oh!
Mako-chan! ♡

Hiya, Chibi-Usa! ♡
I was actually just thinking about dropping by your place!
There's something I want your advice on...

What is it? Acting all formal...
Got some boy on your mind...?
ドキッ
B-BMP
SHE'S SHARP

What ?!
You don't have piripiri or ephedra?? Not even guarana?
My dear shopper, we don't carry such items in this store...

What's going on?
わいわい CLAMOR
わいわい CLAMOR

What about Ipecacuanha? Herb of grace?
Or even allspice?
I-I don't know...
Wait a second...

Are you looking for spices, perhaps?
If so, you can find them at supermarkets that cater to foreigners.

They don't sell spices and herbs at small supermarkets.
Shall I escort you to one of the bigger ones that does?
VWEEN ドライーン
Sunday Sale

Thank you for your kindness, ♡ but...

WINK
...that was actually marketing research, just now.
An herb shop?
HERB SHOP
I just opened today! ♡
It's so thrilling! ♡
I was taking a look around, studying the other stores here in Jûban Shopping District. ♡
Please, come in! ♡
Wow!
I've got just about every kind of herb here.
But my number one pick...
...has got to be this medley of Amazonian medicinal plants.
Ama-zonian?!
BA-BMP
...Don't tell me...

Are you part of the circus?
Yes, I'm a member! ♡
That circus troupe from the Amazon, Dead Moon Circus!
I started a store since it looks like we're going to be here for a while.
Call it a side job.
Piripiri (Cyperaceae family - for menstrual pain)
Ephedra (Ephedraceae family - for bladder inflammation)
Guarana (Sapindaceae family - a cure-all)
Ipecacuanha (Rubiacea family - expectorant)
So the ones you were mentioning earlier are also Amazonian plants?
That's right! They're all medi-cinal.
To own a little shop like this has been my dream...
...since I was quite young.
Jûban is such a fair place. I was able to rent this space very cheaply...
What a great city! I just love it! ♡
But I'll eventually head to another city when the circus continues on its tour.
I dream that I can own shops all across the world some day!

...Oh!

My dream, too... is to own some shops one day.

A florist and a cake bakery.

...B-BMP B-BMP ドキドキ

How wonderful! I hope you accomplish that!

Once you choose your goals, you need to work hard towards them when you are young!

My dear customers,

I offer you special presents for being my very first two visitors!

What a pretty ring!

That is an Amazon Stone.
An Amazonian charm against evil spirits,
it can also make dreams come true.
Oh! Wel-come!
CLANK カラン CLANK カラン
Come in and take a look! ♡

Fresh
Vegetables
Fresh
Fresh
I sliced the tomatoes and put them in the salad!
Mako-chan! ♡
Sprinkle some basil onto it, and then we're done! ♡
Okay!
Basil?
It's an herb that makes tomatoes taste yummier!
Wow! ♡
She was such a lovely and bright person.
Continuing to work hard even after realizing her dream.
...Makes dreams come true, huh? ♡
"You need to work hard when you're young!"
...My dream...
Today's theme is Italian! ♡

...Both my parents died early on, and I've been living on my own for a long time now...
...so I'd like to get married...
...and create a happy household quickly.
And then, open a small flower shop and cake bakery.
This next part's a secret, but...
...truthfully, I also want to grow up to be...
...as pretty as Michiru-san.
And as strong...
...as Haruka-san.
I have so many dreams... but...
...have I...
...really been working hard...
...towards achieving them?

And then,
Mako-chan cooked me lots of dishes that contain herbs.
Although I forgot to ask her about Helios after we ate.
I see.
So...
...this is that Amazon Stone ring with the gem...
...that protects against evil?
Well?
It's pretty, but kinda dodgy, too, giving away such pricey-looking rings for free, don't you think?!
Could I borrow this from you, Chibi-Usa?
Of course! ♡
I'm gonna head home, then.
Mamo-chan?
Feel better, okay?
Make sure to eat.
If you ever want anything, just call. I'll go buy it for you.
Yes, yes.
See ya!
...Amazon Stone, huh...

...I told him

to feel better

just like you asked!

But Mamo-chan still seemed sick.

...I see.

Sorry for the bother, Chibi-Usa.

And thanks.

...Why didn't you go see him? After coming all the way here...

Shush.

...I'm scared that he might...

...reject me...

...again.

...Something's happened, right, Mamo-chan?
HERB SHOP
But you'll tell me...
...eventually, won't you?
CLANK カラン
CLANK カラン
Welcom— Oh!
Hello!
Mind if I take a look around?
Of course not!
Well?
Have you made any progress toward your dream since we last met?

...I can't really discuss this with my friends...

...but I...
...have *a lot* of dreams.

And yet... I'm confused...
...as to which path I really ought to choose?

...If I were to continue being a Sailor Guardian...
...there would continue to be battles...
...and maybe I'd never be able to realize these dreams that I've been hiding inside my heart.
...I keep thinking that the path that I'm currently on is wrong...
...Yikes! What am
saying?

If you're hesitant, why not just stop?
Being a Sailor Guardian, that is.
SHUUU
Eh?!
CHITTER
CACK-CACKLE
HEH HEH HEH
SHUUU
Whoa! What are they?!
CHATTER
CHATTER
CACKLE
This ring! I can't get it off?!
CHIT-CHITTER
My cute little Lemures are...
...incarnations of nightmares, and they desire you, as you're packed so full of dreams you're almost bursting at the seams!
HEH HEH HEH
CACK-CACKLE
Why don't you join the Dead Moon Circus, too, my dear?
SNICKER
Come peddle nightmares with me, all across the world! ♡
CHIT-CHITTER
CACK-CACKLE

SHUUU
SHUUU
Ack!!
GASHANK
GASHANK
The gates ?!

FLAFF
FLAFF
Now no one shall come rescue you, you poor thing. ♡ Heh heh!
SHUUU
This is the Amazon Stone, "Orb Knot."
Just try to undo it, if you can!

SHUUUU
My strength is leaving me...! ...I'm so sorry... every-body...
This time, the Sailor Guardians will be finished for good.
SNICKER SNICKER

What a cakewalk!
GAMPF
...piter...
Jupiter!
OH!
...Where is this?
We're inside your consciousness right now, Jupiter!

PASSH
Oww!
Get a grip! Sheesh!
What are you doing showing weakness to the enemy?!
That's how you got taken advantage of, you know!
Have you forgotten your mission?!
Without monster strength Jupiter around,
who's gonna protect Princess Serenity, Mars, Mercury, Venus, and the others?!
Who's gonna protect the people of this city?!
...That's right...
...I'm "monster strength Jupiter."
I may have lots of dreams...

...but my number one dream right now...
...is to become the strongest Guardian and protect every-one I love...!
And that's my mission, too...!
Makoto, remember this well.
Your greatest enemy, before you defeat any physical foe...
...is your own weakness!
I know, Haruka-san...
...I will not give in!
That's my girl!
Sailor Jupiter!

My Princess Jupiter!
FFT
That is your Jupiter Crystal.
Who *are* you ...?
You could say I'm like a piece of you.
I'm always watching over you.
Go get 'em, monster strength Jupiter!
KAKK
BCCH

Jupiter Crystal Power Make Up!!
GASHAAAN
What the?!
...These are...!
...Oak leaves! The emblem of thunder and light-ning!!

I swear to run you out of this city!
That'll be the day the Dead Moon Circus dies!
FFT
VZZT
VRSSH
VZZZT
Jupiter Oak Evolution!!
FFT

Jupi-
ter?!
Usagi!
Chibi-
Usa!
Heh
heh heh!
Impressive,
Sailor
Guardian!
But you
are going
to be the
ones to
die!!
FFT
AHA HA HA HA
Who are
they?!
CHINGG
BA-BUMP
...The
bell!!
CHINGG
Helios?!

CHING
Helios is calling out to me from somewhere...?!
Mamo-chan?!
BAMM
Mamo-chan!!
CACK-CACKLE
HEH HEH
CACK-CACKLE
CHITTER

Helios!!
Chibi-Usa!
Usagi!
Moon Crisis...

...Make Up!!
PAAAAA

Moon Gorgeous Meditation!!
WHOOSH
FWAA
...Young maiden...
Helios?!

He's wounded all over ...?!
HAHH
はあ
GOFF
ゴボッ
Mamo-chan?!
HAHH
ハア
HAHH
ハア
... Don't look!
BLOP
ボタッ
Mamo-chan?!
...Black blood?!

Pretty Guardian

Sailor Moon

Act 43 Dream 5, Venus Dream

Mamo-
chan!!
Mamoru-
san!!

COUGH
...Black blood?!!
Since when, Mamo-chan?!
Why are you spitting up black blood...?!
...I don't know.
I've been having chest pains for a little while...
HAHH
はあ
And there are black shadows on his lungs...
Helios!
Please tell us!
Helios, you know something, don't you?! Is Mamo-chan's black blood related to you or the enemy?
Did the enemy do this?!

...It appears that we are starting to run out of time.
Very well, I will tell all.
FWAA
...I am...
...Helios, Priest of Elysion.

Helios...
...Priest of Elysion?
Elysion?
Elysion is the sacred land that protects Earth.
It is a place that quietly exists deep inside Earth...
...and is like the heart of this planet.
...I am the priest who serves that place.
My duty...
...is to watch over Elysion, Earth...

...and you, Prince Endymion.
I am also your guardian priest, your Highness.
My guardian priest...?
You are Earth's noble Prince Endymion,
who has been protected by this planet...
...from the ancient past through today.
Prince? You know about me?
Yes, your Highness.
You may not know me, but...

This planet is protected by the sacred land of Elysion,
and my life is also linked to Elysion.
And they are set up
to resonate with each other.
You, this planet,
Elysion, and my-self...
Our four hearts and bodies are all linked.
...four linked...
...hearts and bodies?
That resonate...?

But it was never expected that our link would lead to something like this...
PAAH
POHH
...?!
JAB
FWAA
FWAA
Mamo-chan, what's that inside your chest ...?!

...There's a black rose...
...abloom in my chest...?!
POMH
The inside of my chest, too...
...is infested with this accursed black rose.
It is a sign that Elysion has suffered corrosion.
Your Highness has fallen victim to the same curse that was cast upon Elysion and myself.

What you are seeing right now is just a mirage.
Currently my body...
FLAFF
...has been cursed into the form of a pegasus...
...and has been imprisoned inside Elysion.
...Cursed?! Imprisoned...?!
A black rose...
inside Mamo-chan's chest...?
Curse?!
...But who did these things to you...?!
...There is only one
capable of such feats.

...Queen Nehelenia, ruler of the Dead Moon,
the Kingdom of Nightmares inside the new moon.
Dead Moon is a king-dom...
...sealed deep within the new moon's dark-ness.
They have schemed since ancient times to displace
the Kingdom of Light, Silver Millennium, and rule Earth.
...Dead Moon's queen, Nehe-lenia,
is a spiteful, tenacious monster.
She calculated that this planet would easily fall...
...if damage was inflicted upon Elysion now... with Silver Millennium's shining power from the Moon gone...

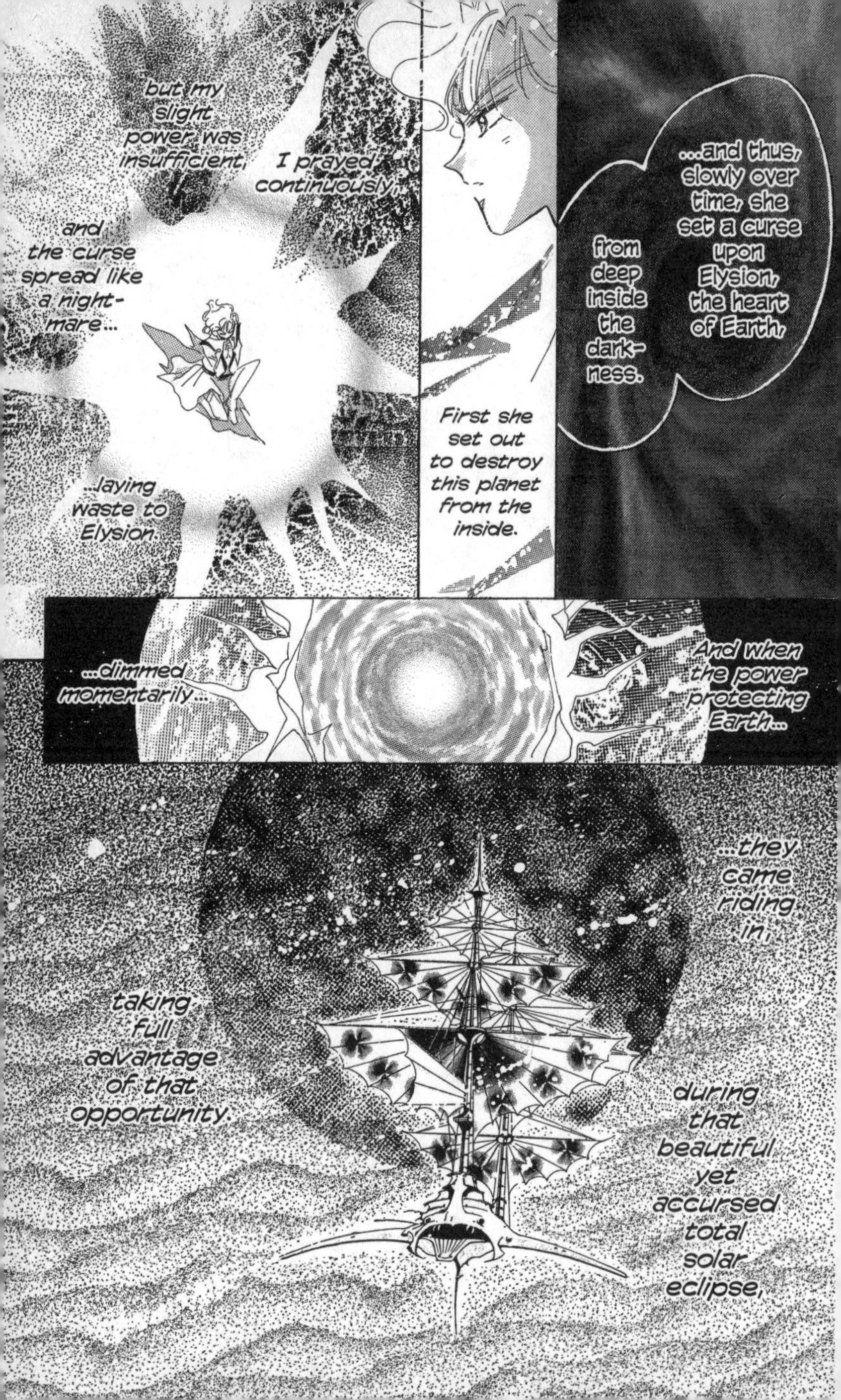
...and thus, slowly over time, she set a curse upon Elysion, the heart of Earth,
from deep inside the darkness.
First she set out to destroy this planet from the inside.
I prayed continuously,
but my slight power was insufficient,
and the curse spread like a nightmare...
...laying waste to Elysion.
And when the power protecting Earth...
...dimmed momentarily...
...they came riding in,
during that beautiful yet accursed total solar eclipse,
taking full advantage of that opportunity.

This planet is currently under attack from both the inside as well as the outside.
Due to their curse,
Elysion is on the verge of death,
oppressed by nightmares and darkness.
If this situation continues to persist...
...nightmares will soon spread across the surface of the planet as well...
...trans-forming it into a planet of death.
And the planet will end up in their possession.
Princess Serenity... or rather, Super Sailor Moon.

They...
...don't seem to have noticed yet that you...
...the successor to Silver Millennium, have returned to life on this planet.
Please defeat them with your power and the power of your "Legendary Silver Crystal!"
Of course! I swear to take the enemy down!
And then, Elysion,
you, and Mamo-chan will all be saved, right?
...Unfortunately...

...although sufficient to defeat the enemy,
the power of the "Legendary Silver Crystal" alone
is not enough to remove the curse upon Elysion and the Prince.
...What do you mean?!
...It was quite a trial for me,
in my weakened condition, to track you and the Prince
down, young maiden.
FLAFF
And then I finally found you.
Princess Serenity... if you truly are the "Chosen young maiden"...
...you ought to be able to locate the Golden Crystal and draw out its power...

..."She who possesses beautiful dreams
...and is protected by the light of the moon."
The chosen young maiden,
who is princess and guardian both,
and bears the sacred gem which undoes the Golden Crystal's seal...
Golden Crystal?
SUU
Helios?!
...Young maiden,
I am a mere priest.
I only possess the power to watch over, pray, and seek help.
FLAFF

Young maiden,
your power is required.
The day that the seal on the Golden Crystal will be undone, has come.
Please use the powers of the "Legendary Silver Crystal" and the Golden Crystal
to save everything from the nightmares...
...!!
PAAA
FFT
Helios!
Without the Golden Crystal,
neither Mamo-chan, Helios...
...Elysion, nor this planet can be saved...?!
This Golden Crystal...

...where is it? How do I look for it...?!

COUGH

Mamo-chan?!

...Don't come near me!

HAAH

はあっ

...This curse...

might spread to you, too!

You shouldn't hang around me...!

I can't help you at all like this...!

...I'm staying put.

Just like how you can feel this planet's pain...

Your pain...
...is my pain.
I swear I'll heal you!
So no matter what...

...let me stay with you!
And tell you that we'll fight this together...!
Usa...!
...I will protect
this planet, this man,
and everyone else...!

Helios...!

I want to help him!

...Neither the Prince nor Elysion can be saved without the Golden Crystal.
...And likely not this planet, either...

This Golden Crystal...!

Where in the world is it?

...What sort of gem could it be?!

...So we need this Golden Crystal in order to fully rescue
Earth from Dead Moon's clutches, huh?

I can't believe Mamoru-san is in such bad shape...!

...We ought to consider this enemy different from any others we've faced.

From this moment on,
we five must help Usagi and protect Mamoru-san as we fight.

...Yup!

MIIIN
ミーン
ミーン
MIIIN
We need to formulate a solid plan
for how we're going to confront...
...the Dead Moon Circus.
Yeah.
...I wish those three were still around.
Huh?
Haruka-san, Michiru-san, and Setsuna-san.
I've been thinking lately...

...that it was thanks to them,
we were able to get a little stronger, after fighting alongside them.
... You know,
there was a short while when I couldn't trans-form...
...but then I thought of Haruka-san, Michiru-san and Setsuna-san,
and I felt my strength build up...
...and was able to power up and trans-form.
Those "mini me's" that appeared during our transfor-mations...
I feel like they might have been...
...messages of encour-agement sent by the three of them.
Right, Mina?
Y-Yup.
Right.
...I've been thinking, lately...

Why am I the only one...

...who can't transform?!

Don't panic. The others said they
weren't able to transform for a while, either!
Then they each sensed a power-up
and encountered pieces of themselves, remember?
This next one is a special transformation!
I bet you're on the verge!
Power worthy of a leader is accumulating inside your body, Mina!
I mean, you *are* the leader of the Sailor Guardians, after all!
You'll be able to transform again in no time!
It's just delayed. I'm sure the time is near!
...right.
Well, I suppose it's not useful to fret over it, so...
I guess I'll go take a bath!
...It's true...
...That's right, this is a very special transformation.
...I sense something coming ...!

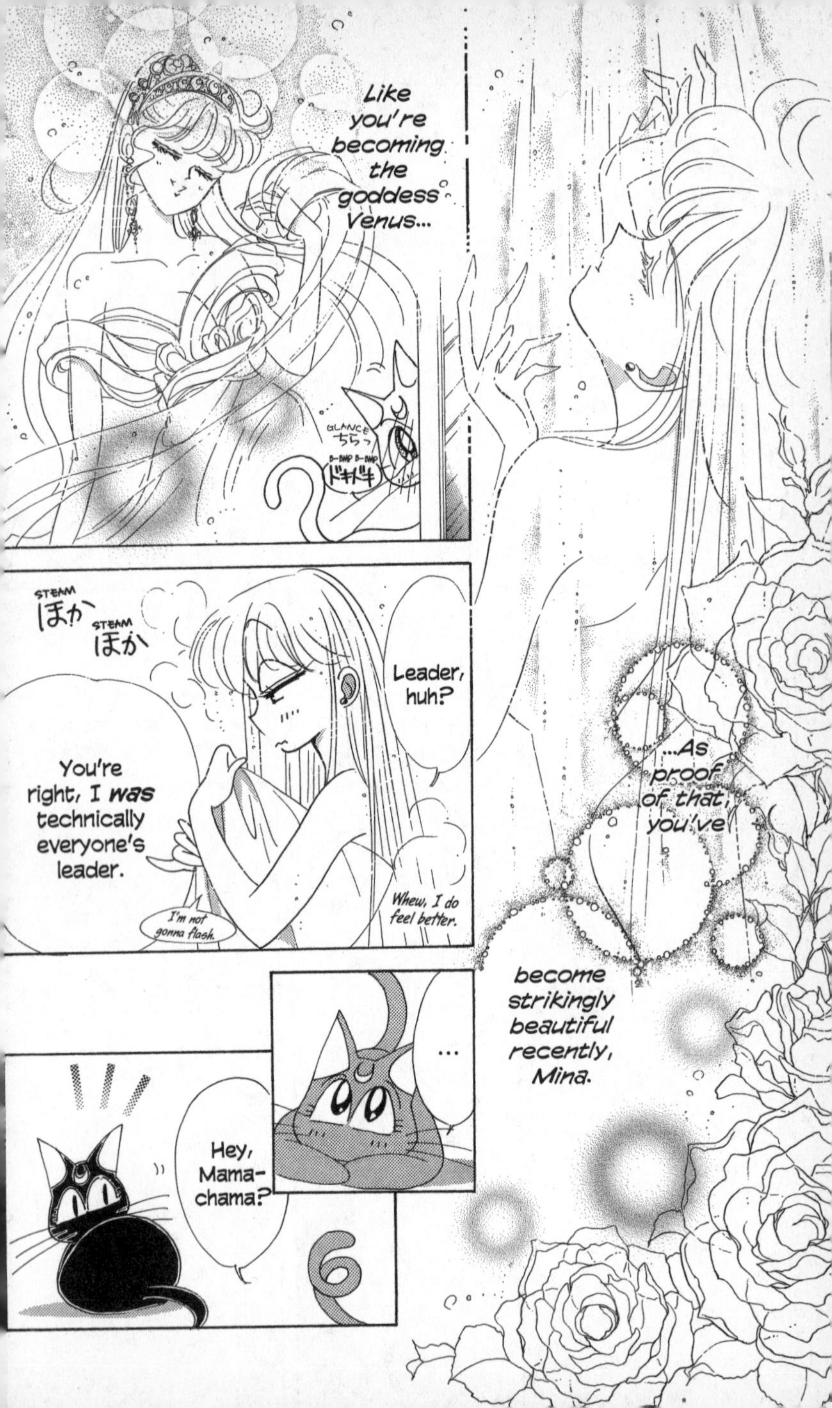
Like you're becoming the goddess Venus...
GLANCE
ちらっ
B-BMP B-BMP
ドキドキ
...As proof of that, you've
become strikingly beautiful recently, Mina.
STEAM
ほか
STEAM
ほか
Leader, huh?
You're right, I was technically everyone's leader.
Whew, I do feel better.
I'm not gonna flash.
...
Hey, Mama-chama?

GAZE
You know, Papa-chama looks at Minako-sama...
...the way one gazes upon his or her lover.

Aw, Diana! ☆
You're so precious!

But I cannot condone you peeping during her bath!!
YOWL
CHOMP

Oh my! ♡
SWIIING
Did you realize there's one
among the Sailor Guardians who can't transform? ♡

In every world, there are always runts, eh?

Spreading nightmares only among the humans at our circus shows is starting to get boring.

Wanna use her to put on a fun event?
Whee! ♡ I vote yes!

SHUU
Zenotime! Zeolite!
SHUU

Let us handle this, ♡ big sisters!
KAKK
We two are not like that dimwitted Amazon trio!

CHITTER CHITTER
Using the Lemures, we shall
not only boost the numbers of night-mares...

...but during the event's climax, we'll
do away with those nuisances, too!
HEH HEH HEH
We shall also obtain this "Legendary Silver Crystal"
that our queen Nehelenia-sama desires!

The four of us are scouting today.
Geez, it's a crazy hot summer this year! ☆
The city seems to be getting more and more roughed up! ☆
Oh dear, a fight?
People are more irritable when it's so hot.
It's escalating! ☆
GYAA
GYAA
Oh! Isn't that ...?
I borrowed Michiru-san's mirror from Chibi-Usa.
That Dead Moon Circus! We need to shut down that tent!
Well?
Shall we launch a surprise attack?!

I was hoping Michiru-san's mirror might pick up some abnormalities.
I've been sensing unrest, not just heat, in the air lately.

A strange aura is enveloping Jûban, with the circus troupe at its center.
It's either a ward, or brain-washing waves.

A ward?!

...Could that be the reason why I'm not able to transform...?
ドキンドキン
BA-DMP
BA-DMP

But it doesn't explain why I'm the only one affected...
Mina?

Oh! no, no, noth-ing.
So you investigated this ward thing on your own, Ami? That's awesome!

Yeah, using a program Setsuna-san gave me.
ピク
PIKK
バ
FWAP
バ
FWAP
バ
FWAP
OH!
は

...When-ever I hear a chopper...
...I just
keep wondering if it might be Haruka-san and the others.
...
FWAP
FWAP
FWAP
Wouldn't we be able to survey things a lot more easily if we could use a chopper for our legwork, like Haruka-san's group?
Just kidding, since none of us have licenses!
...Five.
Huh?
From when we first met up today,
those three's names have been mentioned a total of...
...*five* times!
Well, *I* think it's pointless to think about...
...people who aren't around!

Mina?
It's just that we could rely on them if they were here.
Sure, since I'm such...
...an un-reliable leader!
That's not what we're saying at all!
You're acting weird today, Mina!
Mina?
...So I'm weird.
I'm fine being weird, all right?! Just fine!!
Mina!!

...Ahh, I'm such a loser!
... ポロ PLIP
ポロ PLIP
...Now I've totally disqualified myself as a leader! ☆
...ぐすっ SNIFF
Ahh,
why am I feeling so irritable?
What is up with my power?
Why can't I transform?
If the enemy shows up, how am I supposed to fight like this?!
Blowing her nose
SNIFF ぐっすん
ビーム HONK
Miss.

Won't you consider entering an idol audition?
Snot
You were scouted?!
Yup!
Heh
So, anyways, I've got an audition to head out to now...
...and I swear I'll! Become! An idol!! Like I've always dreamed! ♡
Mina?!
Wait, are you serious?!
...go ahead.

Is it some sketchy production company? Show me the scout's business card!
Dead Moon Enterprises, Inc.
Mr. Xenotime
Dead Moon Enterprises?!
Mina!! Did you look at it?!
I'm off! ♡
Mina?!
ヴィーン VEEEN
I'm not stupid!
I know that this is a Dead Moon trap!
Dead Moon Idol Audition
Applicant Guidelines
Greatest idol in history will be born!!
Feh!
I figured it was too good to be true! Sniff!
Mina! Hold up! Have you lost your mind?! How can you even think about going in there alone,
when you can't transform?!
Shut up!
ムガムガッ MUUG MUUG
This is my chance to demonstrate my power as the leader!
So long as I can still move, I'm going after Dead Moon!

Dead Moon Construction, Inc.
Dead Moon Construction, Inc.
I, Sailor Venus, will combine business and pleasure in my battle!
Dead Moon Idol Audition Venue
Audition Venue
CHATTER
CHATTER
Perhaps 'cuz it's been so sticky lately...
...but this place feels especially stuffy and oppressive.
...When in the world did so many Dead Moon buildings pop up...?!
CLANG
CLANG
Dead Moon Construction, Inc.
Dead Moon Construction, Inc.
No, it's not just heat. There's an odd feel to the air here.
Have they been invading further and further without us knowing it?
...All right! I'm gonna get to the bottom of this!

Audition
TA-DAA
Ehh?! ☆ This many girls are applying?!
...
But then...
...they'll find out that I can't trans-form...!
I can't rescue all these people by myself. I ought to contact Ami-chan and the others...
Attention, everybody! Please come inside the tent that is serving as the audition venue!
WHOOSH
I'll fight them alone! That's what I'd decided, after all!
YEAH
No, Mina! Whining is unacceptable! No matter how weak I am, I'm still a Guardian!

A jungle ?!
CACKLE CACKLE
ケケケケ
CHITTER CHITTER
キキキッ
Now! The Survival Audition begins!
In this audition, you must follow the built-in storyline.
Each of you is to become a hero, traverse the jungle...
...and rescue the children at the top of that tower!
Waah waah!
I'm scared!
How dare they put kids up there!!
To first place shall go 5 million yen* in prize money!
Plus! TV and film lead roles, appearances in commercials, CD releases, and more!!
KYAAAA
きゃあああ～
*5 million yen = approx. $50,000 US.

PAAAAN
パァーン
Ready, set, GO!!
きゃあああああ
KYAAAAAA
ドドドッ
DM DMM
Outta my way!
No, me!
I'm going first!
Ho, ho! ♡ Fight, fight!
Keep releasing more and more energy!
And the Lemures shall transform all that energy and your dreams into nightmares!
Such a massive proliferation of nightmares makes me just giddy! ♡
Calm down, everyone! Something's wrong with this audition!
We need to leave this tent!
Shut up! We're gonna become idols!!
Wait, y'all!!
ドドドッ
DM DM DM

Watch out!!
GLONK
GLONK
?!
Mina! No more of this going solo thing, you hear?!
Jupiter ?!
PAAN
CHIT-CHITTER
CACKLE-CACKLE
Transform, Mina!
Mars?! Mercury?!
That's right! We always fight together!

Venus Planet Power!
Make Up!!
Mina?!
It's no good! I still can't transform!
At this rate, I'll just end up getting in everyone's way!
I'm going on ahead!
Mina!!
ZHAA
ZH-ZHAA
!!

CACK-CACKLE
CHITTER
Hang in there, everybody!!
These guys keep multiplying!
Don't tell me they're sucking up everyone's power?!
CHIT-CHITTER
CACK-CACKLE
Those girls just want to become idols.
How dare their pure and beautiful dreams be used against them!!
ZHAA
How unforgivable! I swear to squash this event, Dead Moon!!

Waah, waah!
HYUUU
SWIS
!!
SWIS
Still a Sailor Guardian despite her disability, huh?
She's managed to make her way here without falling prey to the Lemures!
Waah!
Waah!
HYUUUU
I will rescue them all!!
Mina! Watch out!
!!
KA-KAAK

Now, my dear Lemures, go ahead and eat up these Sailor Guardians!

Ah ha ha ha!

CHITTER

CACK-CACKLE

CRATCH

Yes! I made it! Hold on, everybody, I've come to rescue you!

HYOI

HAAH

Waah!

Waah!

SUUU

FFT
...Shoot! They're not children!!
CACK-CACKLE
CHIT-CHITTER
TUNK
TUNK
Con-grats!
You cleared the numerous obstacles and made it here definitively ahead of all the others!
Now! You're only one step away from idol-hood!
Your last task will be a special treasure hunt!
I can't move!
Darling Lemures-chan! ♡
CHITTER
BWAA
Lemures ?!
CACKLE

Oohoo! ♡
Now you're one of us! A member of Dead Moon!
...Everything's going grey... They're coming inside my head...!
CHITTER
Aieee!
CRACK-CRACKLE
So, go back to your friends and steal...
...the "Legendary Silver Crystal" for us! ♡
キキキッ CHIT-CHITTER
CACKLE
GWUP ... むくっ
WHOOSH
Bring the "Legend-ary...
...Silver Crystal" to us members of the Dead Moon... heh! ♡

Mina!!
SCRATCH
SCRATCH
KYAAA!
Arte-mis?!
Snap out of it, Mina!
Feh!!
STAMP
だんっ
POP
かっ
You're kidding...!
HYUU
HYUU
I'm gonna fall...!!

BYUUU
GRATCH
...It's no use...
My arm feels like it's gonna tear...!!
Hey, let me have some fun here, too, please? ♡
Palla-Palla?!
FFT
Artemis ?!
Orb Hail-storm!!
VATCH
DANGLE

GLITTER
Arte-
mis!!
ZWUU
Artemis!!
NOOO!

Haruka-san, Michiru-san, Setsuna-san...
...and Hotaru-chan...
...That's right...
...we're always trying to pursue you...
...this much...

Act 44 Dream 6,
New Soldiers Dreams

Pretty Guardian
Sailor Moon

"...Surely some revelation is at hand;
Surely, 'the Second Coming' is at hand."
"...'The Second Coming!' Hardly are those words out
When a vast image out of 'Spiritus Mundi'
Troubles my sight:..."
"...Somewhere in sands of the desert
A shape with lion body and the head of a man,
A gaze blank and pitiless as the sun...
...Is moving its slow thighs, while all about it
Reel shadows of the indignant desert birds..."*

**This is an excerpt from William Butler Yeats' The Second Coming*

...My dream, you see...
...is to live happily with the person I love...
...and our child, in a cute house...
...nestled among blooming flowers.

...I wonder if that's...
...what you'd say...
...if I asked you what your dream was?
FWEET
A blue Ferrari... an F512 M!
Twelve cylinders, maximum power of 440 PS, and maximum speed of 315 km/h!
...A super-fast machine that can manipulate wind.
With an apropos "AZZURRO HYPERION" blue metallic body fitting for the wind
...A "blue, roaming Titan'...huh?
Man or wo-man?
...Wo-man!

Hey!
You by your-self?
Want to cruise together for a bit, then grab some tea or some-thing...?
PAA
GACHII
VROM-ROM
...You're 10 billion light years too early...
...to hit on this Haruka-sama!
HYUNN
AIEEEE!!

Um...
RECOMMENDED
Michiru Kaiô-san... right?
Ahh, it really *is* you!
I'm a *huge* fan! I've got all of your CDs!
May I shake your hand?!
Do you come to this CD store often?
Oh! Do you perhaps live near here?
QUIET
HEALING
SUU

GYUUUH
ぎゅうう~
Well, well, thank's a lot for buying all her CDs!
ACK!
Oww ...!!
Sorry for the wait! ♡
Pure white roses?
Nice.
From a fan?
Nope.
Bought them myself.
They're to celebrate the six-month mark since the start of our new life.
...Half a year already, huh?
Look! It's the violinist Michiru Kaiô! She's back in this country?
There'd been a rumor she'd emigrated abroad?!
Is that her boyfriend F1 test driver Haruka Ten'o,
the other half of her red-hot romance? So cool!! I wonder if it's true that they live together?

Look, look! Look at both of their left ring fingers!
No way... They're married?!
VROOOM
Michiru!
A super special on diapers and baby formula! It's a huge bargain!
Sun Pharmacy
Infant Diapers Baby Formula Super special price
500 yen
MU
*500 yen = approx. $5 US.
Haru-ka,
you still haven't broken the habit?
VWON
Our little princess
graduated from formula and diapers long ago, remember?

GASHAAAN
GACHAGACHAAN
WAAAAAN
うわあーーん
Pi
That'd be the kitchen. Aw, geez! ☆
She was quietly reading a book just a minute ago!
I'm begging you, please don't hurt yourself too badly before the other two get home!
WAAANN AAANN
AAAAN
SUUU
We're home ...! ♡
Yikes ...
This summer's heat is *extreme!*
PAUSE
TP
TP
TP
TP

TAA
Haruka-Papa! Welcome home!
Let's continue playing that game from yesterday! ♡
You have your violin lesson with Michiru-Mama today!
Whaaat ?!
Puh-leez! Now, off to your room to change!
...oh no!
SHOCK
My Lalique and Royal Copenhagen plates... smashed.
...Sorry. She was quietly reading a book until just earlier.
Well, it can't be helped. That child finished reading everything in the study a while back.
The other day, she recited one of Virgil's poems from memory.
My eyes almost popped out of my head!

...For sure.
CHUCKLE
It's a trial keeping up with the speed of Hotaru's maturation and development.
I'm gonna wear this today!
Every day is like a dream.
I was totally startled when Hotaru suddenly started growing every day at a scary rate...
SLURP
It's unbelievable how big she's gotten in just half a year.
Good to go!
Indeed.

Today marks exactly six months
since we started this new life...
I also feel like I've been dreaming all this time.
She was so quiet and obedient back when we were still changing her diapers, that I can't believe what a naughty imp she is now!
By the way...
In charge of manners and schooling
Manages meals and health care
Diapers and playmate
KICK KICK
ばたばた
...Yeah, for sure...
...every day really has seemed like a dream...
...Even that eclipse...
...That total solar eclipse
that occurred a few weeks after we four started living together.
...That day,
I was performing observations at the Tokyo Bay Astronomical Observatory.

First contact = start of a solar eclipse

First contact... confirmed.

ピッ

ピッ

The first bad vibe... since the start of our new life.

...I'd had an ominous premonition.

Total Solar Eclipse

A Once in a 1000 Year Event

News-paper

Japan

...ドキ BA-BMP

...ドキ BA-BMP

Please, I pray that nothing happens.

Second contact... confirmed.

Second contact = start of a total solar eclipse

!!
CHIT-CHITTER
CACK-CACKLE
HEH HEH HEH
...-san?
Se-tsuna-san?
OH!
CHATTER CHATTER
You're drenched in sweat!
The total solar eclipse
has ended uneventfully.
Un-eventful?!
Oh, no, not at all!
The airspace distorted for an instant!
No one else felt it?!

...Something's invaded from another plane...!
An enemy?! I must look into it!
I'll transform and investigate!
Pluto Planet Power...
Make Up!!
?!
I can't transform?!
...tsuna-Mama?
はっ
OH!
Setsuna-Mama?

It's noth-ing.
Sorry.
...half a year already.
...It's not like we didn't know.
The battle ended that day.
And we three chose to go separate ways.
...The fact that I can't transform is likely a sign that our mission has ended...
...And yet...
...starting the day after that eclipse...
...you began growing daily with fearsome speed, before our very eyes, Hotaru.
Hotaru, is this power of yours... a sign that you are going to awaken?

Good.

Well done.

Okay, next up is Hotaru-chan.

... Three.

Begin.

Here it comes!

WHISPER

GIGGLE

FWAA

There it is!
The pegasus ghost!!
WHOA
KYAAA
Sensei! There it is again! We saw that ghost last week too, right?!
Why does it appear when Hotaru-chan starts playing?
Quiet, every-one...!
Nooo, I'm scared!
FWAA
WHOA
A girl!
... That's...
...Small Lady?!
!
PATTER PATTER
ぱたぱた

Wait!
Hotaru?!
TAA
NEIIIGH

Just like Saturn's...
FFT
フッ...
...I've seen that girl before.
She was in a photograph together with Michiru-Mama.
She was crying...
...just now. Because that pegasus had died.
Poor thing...

Is she...
...perhaps
going to awaken again?
Goodbye, Michiru-sensei!
Bye-bye, Hotaru-chan!
Bye-bye!
GAZE じっ
CHUCKLE くすっ
...Now, shall we have dinner?
Yay!

...If we could only live...
...together in this house forever...
...However...
...my heart feels uneasy.
The day when we will wake
from this dream...
...is approaching...

Is your game of nurturing the solar system progressing smoothly?
Just what is your role, Haruka?
On its own, Hotaru's power will run wild, so I'm acting as a "check" to control her power.
Wow ...!
All those planetesimals that existed just yesterday have completely disappeared!
The gas is rapidly dissi-pating, too...
We're simulating our solar system's entire life history at high speed.
And now we've reached today, 4.6 billion years later, with it in its current form.

Those tiny flashing lights.
What are they?
FLICKER
FLICKER
FLICKER

Minor planets that were birthed... absent their own volition...
Lights puzzling over whether to live or die.

...Isn't this white glow...
...the moon?
...So pretty. Just like a pearl.

It's as if the light is wrapping around the blue glass bead that is Earth.
Haruka-saaan!

The same light that always surrounded that girl.
Haru-ka...?!
...I want to see her.
ZHAAA
RUMBLE
I wonder... if they're all doing well.
...We just hit that total solar eclipse from a few months ago.
ZHAAA!!
!!
PAAA

...Wait! Earth is turning blacker and blacker...!
But I thought the eclipse was over...?!

...The moon's glow...
SUUU
スゥッ
... became pitch black...!

Hotaru!
はっ OH!
PANN
PANN

...Why don't we call it quits for today.
ZHAA

Off to bed after you take your bath.
Okay.

TAA
タッ

Earth and Moon enveloped
in darkness after the total solar eclipse...
That was the vision Hotaru saw, right?
ZHAAA

The space-time flux that appeared in the skies above Tokyo,
the abnormal elevation in temper-ature,
the unusual prolifer-ation of vegatation every-where...
...and the inexplicable decay of cities—
—I've since discovered that it's all being controlled by the new moon.
ZHAAA

Plus, these strange phenomena only started after that total solar eclipse...!
There's been an enemy invasion!
I know that already, Setsuna!
But...
...that day, you at the Tokyo Bay Astronomical Observatory...
...me, during a performance
in Vienna later on...
...and during a race in Africa...
We all sensed an enemy shadow within the cities and people,
enveloped in darkness and starting to decay.
But none of us were able to transform!

...We can't transform anymore!
We no longer possess the power of Outer Solar System Guardians!
...Meaning we're no longer considered necessary.
Our princess
has given up on us.
...And the others can
go forth and battle just fine on their own, without us.
They're able
to protect the princess.
...The fact that we can't transform,
it means...

ZHAAA
...we're not needed.
Isn't that so...?
KAKK
KYAA!
RUMBLE RUMBLE
FLINCH

...Don't be scared!

ZHAM

...Who?

...The time of awakening has come...!

ZAWAA
The start of a
new mission.

... Awaken...

...my sleeping soul who protects my planet Saturn...!

...I'm seeing...

...so many visions...

BA-BMP

...We need to hurry!

BA-BMP

ZABAA
ザバーッ

RUMBL RUMBL
ゴロゴロ
SUII
スーイッ

RUMBLE RUMBLE
ゴロゴロ
The COLLECTED POEMS of W.B. YEATS

..."The darkness drops again; but now I know
RUMBLE RUMBLE
…ゴロゴロ
That twenty centuries of stony sleep
Were vexed to nightmare by a rocking cradle..."*
カタッ
KATINK
Hotaru?

*This is another except from William Butler Yeats' The Second Coming.

...A person starts to live when he can...
KACHAK
カチャ

...live outside himself...

KAKK
カッ

Those were Albert Einstein's words.
...Your
appearance...!
ふわっ FWAA
...The time has come.
The time for our new awakening.

No matter how many times we are reborn...
...the person for whom we live is always...
...the same.
...You've regained them?
Your memories of the past ...?!
Ho-taru ...!
You mean ...?!

We are no longer who we were before.
ザラッ
SHFFF

We no longer need to fight individually, from afar.

The four of us...
...were completely reborn anew that day, along with our Princess.

And now, the time has finally arrived.

Thanks for raising me up to this point,
Haruka-Papa, Michiru-Mama, and Setsuna-Mama!
From this point on, it's *my* turn to lead *you three!*
SST
FFT
PAAA
Back to the others!

PAAAA
Here are our Crystals, the sign that...
...we are new Guardians.
FFT
PAAA
...the Holy Grail?!
WAVR
... Prince!
Prin-cess?!

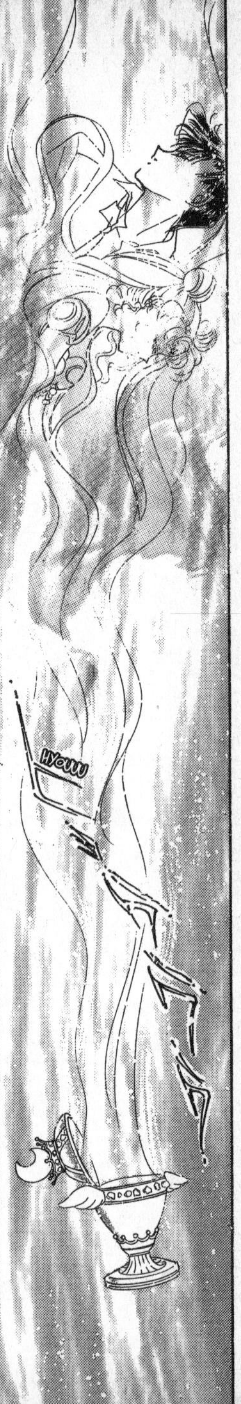

...The two of them don't seem quite right!

What in the world is this...?! What's going on?!

SST

SHUUUU

...The rose changed...!

PLINK

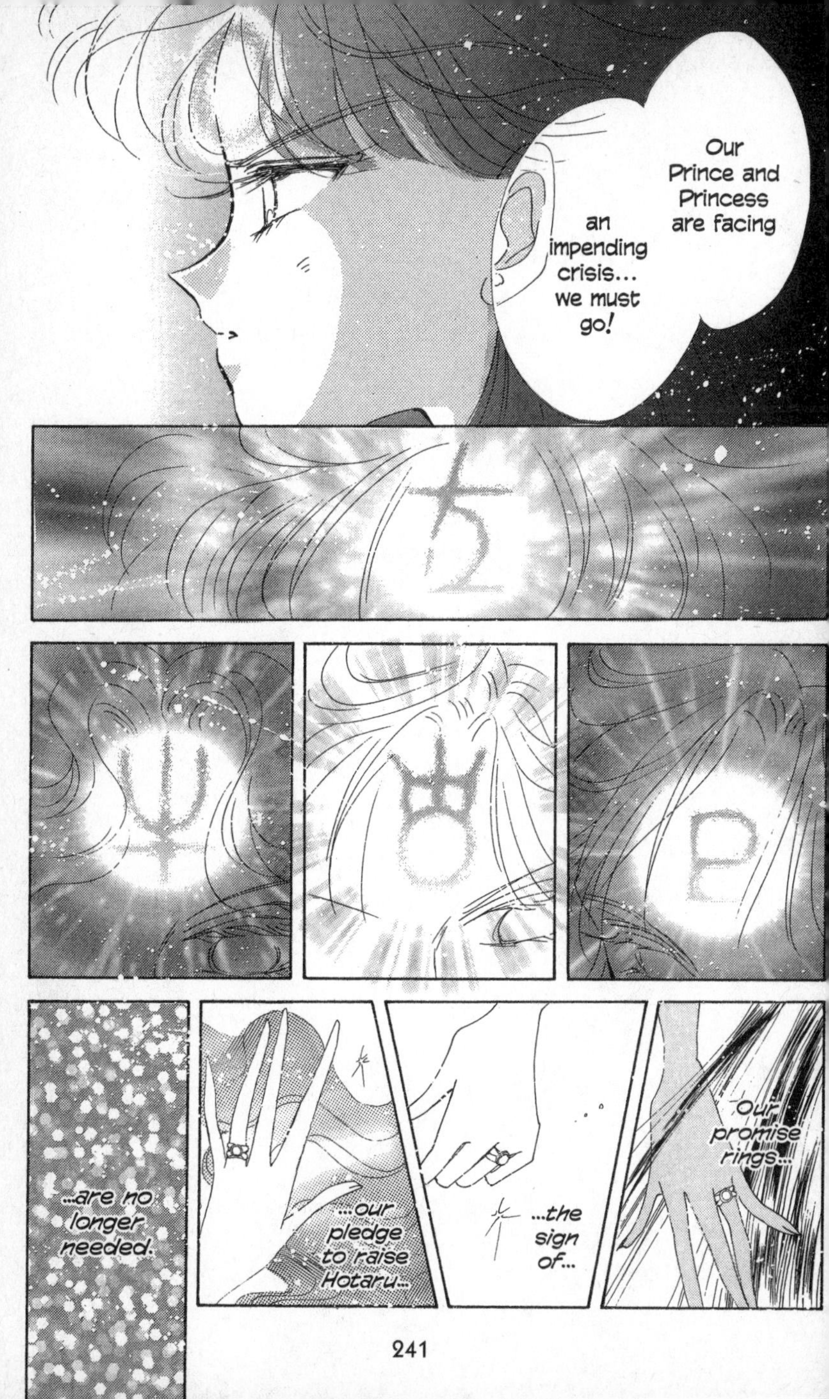
Our Prince and Princess are facing an impending crisis... we must go!
Our promise rings...
...the sign of...
...our pledge to raise Hotaru...
...are no longer needed.

Let's go!
To the place we are meant to gather.
For that is where
our true dreams have always resided, anyway.

Artemis
...!

I'm sorry, Artemis...!

I finally get it. With my whole body hurting so badly right now, in so much pain.

Artemis! We were always of one body and one soul! You're actually a part of me...!

I'm always saying such horrible things to you,

and teasing you.

GURAA

FLINCH
びくっ

GWUP
…むくっ

...I just realized it, too.
HAAH
はあっ

Mina, the reason why you couldn't transform...

SHFFF
サラッ

...is because I, your partner, lacked sufficient power!

...Arte-
mis?
GRIN
…ニコッ
...I feel power swelling up and filling every inch of me!
Artemis and I...
...are linked...
...more strongly than before.

PAAA
PAAAA
FWAH
This is your Venus Crystal, Mina.
Now transform!
Venus Crystal Power...

...Make Up!!
TMP
NOD
Venus!
Arte-mis!

You!!
How dare you torture me, the Goddess of Love and Beauty, Venus-sama, over and over, and treat me like trash!
Take this, Venus' invincible whip of love!!
Venus Love and...

...Beauty Shock!!
ザバあぁっ
!!
FFT
WHOOSH
How dare you!
SHA-SHA
?!

Mercury! Mars! Jupiter!
Venus!
PISHIII
ギャああ!
VWATCH!

Venus!! You were able to transform!
Sorry to have been a bother!
But every-thing's okay now!
All thanks to you, Artemis!
Mina!
No!
ZAA

This is our big event!
We, the Amazoness Quartet...
...shall liven up this party!
Palla-Palla!
I know, Cere-Cere!
Orb Creepers!!
ZW ZW ZW ZW
GRATCH
KYAAAA!!

We are descendants of Amazonesses, the legendary ultimate warriors of the Amazon!
The Amazoness Quartet!!
The dense jungle and sweltering nights of the Amazon...
...and the cursed gems handed down among us Amazoness,
SNICKER
the Amazon Stones...
We have yet to show you the true power of the darkness of the new moon! ♡
SNICKER
HEH HEH HEH クククッ
CACKLE ケケッ
CHITTER キキッ
No!!
WHOOSH
Amazoness Quartet?!

...In order to defeat the enemy and protect those precious to us!
CHITTER
Heh heh heh
Everybody?!
Hang in there, everyone!
CACKLE
Artemis!!
Mina!
...is just my strength alone still not enough?!
Do we still lack sufficient power?!
Heh heh heh
...If we only had more!
Aha ha ha

Power, come to me!!
はっ
OH!

...I feel uneasy.
Is this also the enemy's doing? Their darkness has spread so much that the stars are obscured?
That black spot is the area where you were just earlier...
SHIVVER
Once again tonight, not a single star is visible.
Helios...
I am imprisoned.
I want to go see him.
...I want to go rescue him right now.
But where are you, Helios?
Where is Elysion?!

● to be continued ●

ranslation Notes

panese is a tricky language for most Westerners, and translation is often more art than ence. For your edification and reading pleasure, here are notes on some of the places ere we could have gone in a different direction with our translation of the work, or ere a Japanese cultural reference is used.

ack Lady (page 009.5)
en PallaPalla's Orb Inversion causes Chibi-Usa and Usagi witch physiques at the end of volume 8, Chibi-Usa dvertently ends up resembling her evil alter ego Black y from volume 5.

Guts (page 051.3)
A "guts pose" is essentially the Japanese semantic equivalent of the English"fist pump."

sband (page 072.2)
ere is a centuries-old tradition in Japan of well-to-do families with no or only female children to opt a male adult to carry on the family name and business. When there are no heirs at all (or no pable male heirs), the individual may be a younger male blood relative such as a nephew or cond cousin, who then weds outside his adopted family. In cases (such as Rei's) where there are y daughters, the man is usually a non-relative who takes the adopting family's surname and marries (oldest) daughter.

The fact that I can't kick this fever must mean I'm approaching my end... Namu Amida Butsu*...
MUTTER MUTTER
UNGH
ラーん
らーん
UNGH
...Grandpa, we're a Shinto shrine, not a Buddhist temple...

Namu Amida Butsu (page 074.2)

'Namu Amida Butsu" is a phrase chanted in Japanese Pure Land Buddhist traditions. It means "total eliance upon the compassion of the Amida Buddha," and it is thought that mindful cyclic repetition of this mantra would help cancel out one's negative karma and allow rebirth in the Amida Buddha's pure land or "Realm of Bliss," a refuge from the sufferings of existence where one can attain enlighten-nent. In this respect, it is somewhat similar to the Christian "Hail Mary." What is ironic and the crux of he joke here is that Rei's grandfather is the head of a Shinto shrine, yet is reciting a Buddhist mantra when he thinks he is on his deathbed.

Charms (page 074.4)

raditionally in Japan, charms are sold at both temples and shrines and dedicated to particular Buddhist figures or Shinto deities, respectively. They are considered talismans that confer either luck, protection, or both, upon the individual carrying it or the object it is placed within such as a car or apartment), and are often given as gifts or souvenirs. While most often a small rectangular brocade bag with a string loop, they can come in various other shapes and forms, including bumper stickers and igurines. Specific protections include warding evil, financial luck, traffic or ravel safety, good grades and examination results, commercial prosperity, omantic or marital bliss, safe pregnancy and birth, and physical protection of a household against theft, fire, etc. They are technically supposed to be eplaced yearly, with the old charms brought back to the shrine or temple o be ritually disposed of (usually by fire). These days, one can get secular harms with one's favorite cartoon or anime characters that are considered ashion statements rather than divine protection.

...This is...
...my Mars Arrow!!

Mars Arrow (page 095.2)

Often called "exorcising bows and arrow as well, sacred bows and arrows are par of Shinto tradition, used to dispel evil fro and/or purify an object. As such, the Mar Arrow is an apropos weapon for Rei. The days, one can purchase a version of such arrows from a shrine to protect one's hor much like the aforementioned charms.

‹t of herbs and their properties (page 124.2)

‹ile guarana is definitely native to the Amazon and ipecacuanha is found in Brazil, this translator ‹s unable to confirm where the first two listed herbs originate. In addition, in modern medicine, ‹cac is more known as an emetic and is actually no longer recommended by physicians.

Amazon Stone (page 125.6)

Amazon Stones actually exist, although they aren't found in the Amazon. Amazon Stone" is another name for Amazonite, a green feldspar variety. It has a bright green color but does fractures easily, so Mamoru shouldn't assume it's an ordinary stone just because it shattered when he applied pressure on it.

cada cries (page 168.1)

‹adas are relatively large insects that make distinctive loud sounds. In Japan, their image and/or songs are ‹ed in poetry, television, anime, manga, and other media as a seasonal signifier for late summer (mainly July). ‹re, two different calls "miiin miiin" and "jiii jiii" are "heard," indicating the presence of two separate cicada ‹ecies (each species has a unique song).

chama" (page 172.5)

‹hama" is baby speech for the honorific "-sama," used to indicate the young age of the person (or in this ‹se, animal) speaking.

Pretty Guardian Sailor Moon volume 9 is a work of fiction. Names, characters, places, and incidents are the products of the author's imagination or are used fictitiously. Any resemblance to actual events, locales, or persons, living or dead, is entirely coincidental.

A Kodansha Trade Paperback Original.

Published in the United States by Kodansha Comics, an imprint of Kodansha USA Publishing, LLC, New York.

Publication rights for this English edition arranged through Kodansha Ltd., Tokyo.

First published in Japan in 2004 by Kodansha Ltd., Tokyo, as *Bishoujosenshi Sailor Moon Shinsoban*, volume 9.

ISBN 978-1-61262-005-3

Printed in Canada

www.kodanshacomics.com

9 8 7 6 5 4 3 2

Translator/Adapter: Mari Morimoto
Lettering: Jennifer Skarupa

TOMARE!

STOP

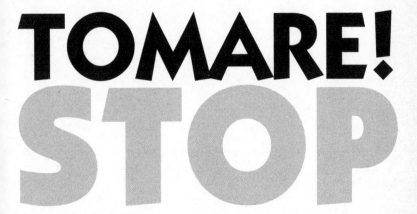

You're going the wrong way!

Manga is a completely different type of reading experience.

To start at the beginning, Go to the end!

That's right! Authentic manga is read the traditional Japanese way—from right to left, exactly the opposite of how American books are read. It's easy to follow: Just go to the other end of the book and read each page—and each panel—from right side to left side, starting at the top right. Now you're experiencing manga as it was meant to be!

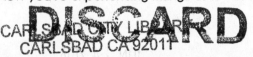